AMERICA'S CUP®
SAN FRANCISCO
THE OFFICIAL GUIDE

INTRODUCTION BY
Roger Vaughan

WRITTEN BY
Kimball Livingston

WITH CONTRIBUTIONS BY
James Boyd and Ivor Wilkins

INSIGHT
EDITIONS

San Rafael, California

CONTENTS

The crew had felt the bows dig in before .

They were familiar with the sensation of the sterns rising out of the water as the bows buried under tons of water rushing past at up to 40 knots.

Turning downwind, or bearing away in the new America's Cup catamaran class requires nerves of steel. It's when the towering, powerful wing sail is broadest to the wind. Every piece of equipment on the yacht strains under the added pressure of the wind against the broad surface area. It's a moment that puts an empty feeling in the pit of the stomach of the sailors—a weird, unsettling sensation that catches one's attention.

The ORACLE TEAM USA crew became acutely aware that this turn downwind had strayed from the norm when skipper Jimmy Spithill yelled, "Keep an eye on your mates!" Moments later, many of the 11 sailors aboard were quite literally swimming for their lives. Shoreside video of the pitch-pole/capsize of *ORACLE TEAM USA 17* shows the incident occurred in no more than 30 seconds. Hours later, as the overturned platform was being

swept westward into a setting sun by an ebb tide, the team could still be seen struggling to recoup all that they could from the once sleek 72-foot "cat."

The 2013 America's Cup is an ambitious attempt to change the event. Every facet of the centuries-old event has been rethought. A new design rule that features, for the first time, wing sail catamarans. The powerful, light boats demand a new breed of sailor; physical prowess and vast reserves of courage are the new currency. The use of a catamaran and its shallow draft allows the racecourse to be placed close to shore, in plain view of spectators sitting in shoreside bleachers or on rocky outcrops. The racing has even been made more appealing to the television viewer, with graphics indicating positioning overlaid in real time on the broadcast picture.

The changes have been met with great fanfare at America's Cup World Series regattas, turning skeptics into supporters. The 2013 America's Cup stands to shatter the mold.

EXTREME SPORT

BY ROGER VAUGHAN

IN 1820,
A STRANGE THING HAPPENED.

A man named John Cox Stevens took delivery of a catamaran he had commissioned as his private yacht. He named it *Double Trouble*.

THIS WAS NOTEWORTHY because private yachts were a rarity in 1820. Catamarans in those days were even rarer. It turned out to be a significant event, because in 1844 Stevens would found the New York Yacht Club and become its first commodore. In 1850, he would become the driving force behind the syndicate that caused the schooner *America* to be designed, built, and sailed across the Atlantic to challenge the British to a boat race. After *America* won that race, he would rename the large silver ewer he won "The America's Cup" and take the lead in writing a deed of gift for a yacht race inviting "friendly competition between foreign countries."

In several ways, John Cox Stevens solidly set the stage for the past 162 years of America's Cup competition that would culminate in 2013 with a match between 72-foot catamarans. First of all, the whole concept of *America* was outrageous. In 1851, not only were the British perceived to rule the waves militarily and in yachting, but also a scant thirty-seven years had passed since they burned Washington, D.C., during the War of 1812. Stevens was a successful businessman from a prominent family. A known gambler, he was by all accounts a smart, aggressive, confident man. And he had an agenda: to promote the design and shipbuilding prowess of the United States. Stevens cut the path for men of his ilk to follow, and follow they did through thirty-three challenges. Without exception, those who have sought to fund competitions for the America's Cup have been among the wealthiest and most powerful individuals in the world, from England's iron and steel baron James Ashbury, the Earl of Dunraven, and aviation pioneer T. O. M. Sopwith to Ireland's tea magnate Thomas Lipton, Italy's fashion maestro Patrizio Bertelli, and Australia's real estate tycoon Alan Bond. American defenders have included familiar names like Vanderbilt, Cunningham, Turner, Koch, and Ellison.

» **PAGES 2-3** *ORACLE TEAM USA 17* gliding along just outside a fog line hugging San Francisco's waterfront. » **PAGES 4-5** "It's a wild untamed beast," said Emirates Team New Zealand tactician Ray Davies when asked about the team's first AC72. And while the team's first big catamaran set the bar high, their second, pictured here, raised it even higher right out of the gates. » **PAGES 8-9** On board ORACLE TEAM USA's AC45. The Golden Gate Strait in the distance reliably funnels strong and chilly ocean winds. » **BELOW** Luna Rossa's AC72 under construction in New Zealand. » **OPPOSITE** ORACLE TEAM USA inspecting wing one of three during an early AC72 training session in October 2012.

Catamarans have relied on the development of new materials and expanding technology to become the ever-faster and more efficient vessels of the last twenty years.

Then there was Stevens's catamaran, *Double Trouble*. Even the name had a challenging, slightly foreboding ring to it. And it was uncannily prophetic.

////////////

CATAMARANS HAVE RELIED on the development of new materials and expanding technology to become the ever-faster and more efficient vessels of the last twenty years. That Stevens was experimenting with multihulls nearly two hundred years ago is extraordinary. Those who imagine that our stuffy forebears in their starched turnover collars and padded frock coats would be horrified at the sight of multihulls racing for the America's Cup need to reconsider. The original Deed of Gift they wrote is remarkable for both its brevity and its latitude. The authors left the doors wide open for innovation and creativity in the quest for speed. Let us not forget that their challenger, *America*, was a very

radical design by the standards of the day. The Americans' intent was to outfox the British at their own game—and that they did. If that group of nattily attired, hard-charging, early-day yachtsmen could look out over San Francisco Bay and watch 72-foot catamarans flying past at 35 knots, their smiles would be as broad as the Cheshire Cat's. (The deed Stevens wrote called for racing on "ocean courses free of headlands," which does not fit San Francisco Bay. But the clever and enterprising Stevens would surely have made an exception for television.)

Those smiles wouldn't have materialized instantly. It would have taken a moment for the shock to wear off. Because even for those of us who have had America's Cup fever since the Cup was restarted in 12-Meters in 1958, shock has been a factor. Tradition can be glorious, tradition is comforting, but "every tradition grows ever more venerable . . .

the reverence due to it increases with every generation," as Friedrich Nietzsche wrote. So when sailors heard the news that the 2013 America's Cup was going to be sailed in multihulls, resistance was the initial gut reaction.

Embracing tippy racing multihulls that skim the surface and are more at home on a beach than at a dock was a tough order for traditionalists. For 152 years, the America's Cup was contested in monohulls that rarely pushed the speed dial over 14 knots. Although there have been gear failures (spars breaking, sails tearing—even a sinking), no boat in the Cup's history has ever capsized. With two notable exceptions aside, for more than 160 years, the Cup has been the epitome of traditional yachting. For many of those years, it was complete with white flannels, navy yachting jackets, gold braid on the caps, and the observation of flag etiquette.

////////////

FROM THE OUTSET, the 2013 America's Cup had an entirely new look. For all their speed and flash, large racing multihulls simply do not have the elegant, often majestic presence of monohulls. With hard wing sails emblazoned with eye-catching logos, with the wide stance of twin hulls that seem too frail, the boats have an experimental look. Wearing heavy-weave, flexible body suits, crash helmets, and life vests that look like pads under form-fitting tops, the crews resemble a cross between mountain climbers and bicycle racers. To those who had followed the event even in a casual way, the new America's Cup was as unrecognizable (unthinkable!) as the advent of blue courts, yellow balls, and colorful outfits were to those used to the green grass, red clay, and white balls and outfits of tennis.

We can't say we weren't forewarned. The multihull with which San Diego responded to the rogue New Zealand challenge in 1988 was a harbinger of things to come, although few realized it at the time. After the long and unpleasant litigation that preceded a ludicrous, one-sided match on the water, the San Diego Yacht Club wrote a protocol to forestall future rogue challenges. But a critical, game-changing precedent had been set. After putting the Deed of Gift under a legal microscope, the New York Supreme Court had, in 1988, allowed a multihull to compete in the America's Cup. On

» LEFT Emirates Team New Zealand's Grant Dalton sprints across the netting of the team's AC72 during an early training session on the Hauraki Gulf in New Zealand.

the water, San Diego's 60-foot, wing sail catamaran made New Zealand's 120-foot monohull look as if it were dragging a giant bucket. That's how much faster a catamaran is than a monohull. The cat gave away 60 feet and sailed rings around New Zealand's "Big Boat." The writing was on the wall: The essence of the America's Cup has always been speed.

It wasn't until twenty years and five Cup matches in monohulls, after the San Diego event, that the multihull issue came up again. Two unique aspects of the America's Cup are that the winner picks the location for the next defense, and he also writes the sailing instructions. This would be unthinkable in other sports, but without the presence of a much-needed permanent America's Cup management authority (akin to the NFL, NBA, and NHL league offices), this tradition prevails. As one might expect, the winner of the Cup has always tilted the playing field a few degrees in his favor. But in 2007, after beating challenging New Zealand in a widely acclaimed, well-contested match held in Valencia, Spain, Team Alinghi's boss, Ernesto Bertarelli, issued a notice of race for his next defense that went several steps over the line. The Challenger of Record, BMW ORACLE Racing run by Larry Ellison, CEO of ORACLE, had no choice but to file legal objections. Two long years of legal wrangling went on between two of the world's wealthiest men. The most proficient attorneys available pitted their skills against one another. Ellison ultimately won fourteen out of fifteen judgments from the New York Supreme Court, though the match was settled on the water, not in the courtroom.

Ellison and Bertarelli still could not agree on the terms for the match. The parties had not settled on a boat, or even a formula for a boat to be used in the competition. When that impasse occurs, the Deed of Gift dictates the particulars. The resulting event is called a DOG (Deed of Gift) match. The boats must conform to a clause in the deed: Competing vessels "if of one mast shall not be less than 44-feet, nor more than 90-feet on the load water-line." The deed specifies the exact nature of courses for a three-race series.

Ellison and his troops were well into preparing a 90-foot waterline monohull for the match initially set for 2009 when they read a headline in the December 11, 2007, *Tribune de Genève*: "Alinghi will defend in a multihull." That's when it all changed. The lesson learned in 1988 was plain: One simply doesn't elect to sail a monohull against a multihull.

The story, still untold at this point, of how BMW ORACLE Racing scrapped its monohull project, refocused a bunch of monohull sailors on the theory and prac-tice of racing multihulls, and recruited help from the best multihull sailors in the world, and how designers and build-ers took on a mission impossible to con-ceive and construct a large multihull in a fraction of the time that would be nor-mally allotted for a project of that size—a 113-foot length overall multihull that would be competitive and also manage-able for a crew of eight mere mortals—is almost beyond belief.

As if that weren't enough, a wing sail was added to the picture only six months before the match was to take place. Not only a wing sail, but at 223 feet, also the tallest one ever built.

Even with aerospace engineers and designers on the team, BMW ORACLE was cautiously exploring uncharted ter-ritory—and under a crippling time con-straint. The learning curve was nearly vertical, and it scratched the sky. Design-ing and building hulls and structural ele-

ments for the platform was tough enough. For the wing, they got help from Boeing engineers and from designers who had been on the 1988 San Diego project. Build-ing a wing was one thing; learning to sail with it was another. Then there was the job of putting it on and taking it off the boat, stepping and unstepping the enor-mous thing that wanted to fly the moment it was lifted off its low, horizontal resting place under a protective tent. Rudders and the bowsprit were redesigned many times, and the foils, or daggerboards— "dagger foils"—were a monumental design project in themselves. The foils for the big multihull were 20 feet long, 6 inches thick where they exited the hull (enough to sus-tain a 20-ton side load), and 3 feet wide. Designers figured the right set of foils was worth 40 minutes around a 20-mile course.

As for the sailing, it was on the edge. Dangerous. Crews wore hard hats with reason. Things kept falling off the wing. Every time they sailed, something broke or malfunctioned. One sailor said he was much more frightened on the big multihull than he had been racing in a Volvo Ocean Race 60-footer when his boat nearly sank under him one dark night. If that big mul-tihull had ever tipped over and gone up on one hull with the top of the wing in the water, the sailors on the raised hull would have been 90 feet off the water—a nine-story drop into the wing, onto the other hull or a winch, or, if they were lucky, into the water. The first time the big multihull ever successfully sailed around the entire America's Cup course was the first race of the 2010 Cup match. The second time was the second race. BMW ORACLE won both races and the Cup thanks in part to the wing sail. Defender Alinghi had used conventional sails.

But the racing was, undeniably, tre-mendously exciting. For viewers, watching

» **ABOVE** BMW ORACLE Racing's huge trimaran during the final match of the 2010 America's Cup.

those 2010 races from Valencia streaming on YouTube was to be on the edge of their seats. Neither race was ever in doubt. The BMW ORACLE trimaran sailed higher and faster upwind than Alinghi's cat, and considerably faster downwind as well. But the tension, the drama of the event, was provided by the mere presence—the performance—of two enormous, immensely powerful vessels that seemed to defy what was thought to be possible. One half expected they might self-destruct at any moment. The sailors were glad when it was over, but all of them still get the tingles when they think back on the speed, the acceleration, that 223-foot wing towering above them . . . the whole amazing, outrageous, frightening craziness they were a part of.

//////////

WELCOME TO EXTREME SAILING. Welcome to the America's Cup as extreme sport. As the old song asks, "How you gonna keep 'em down on the farm after they've seen Paree?" The answer is, you aren't. How can any committed racer of sailboats be satisfied with sailing at 10 knots upwind in a monohull when he can go 16-plus knots upwind in a multihull? How can that sailor be happy going a maximum of 15 knots downwind in an America's Cup monohull when he can be scorching along at 40 downwind in a multihull? He can't. It was a no-brainer when it came to deciding whether to go back to racing monohulls in the 2013 Cup. When BMW ORACLE Racing's CEO, four-time America's Cup winner Russell Coutts, announced that the boat of choice would be a 72-foot catamaran, it was no surprise.

Given that only two teams had gone through a very expensive crash course that had advanced multihull/wing technology to a whole new level, defender BMW ORACLE Racing found itself in the unusual position of having to bring potential challengers up to speed. To do so, the AC45 catamaran was quickly conceived, designed, built, and sold to teams contemplating a challenge. There were nine takers (Alinghi was not among them). A schedule of AC45 racing was announced that saw teams racing for two years at locations beyond the 2013 host venue. Called the America's Cup World Series (ACWS), events took place in Portugal, England, Italy, and the United States. The events included fleet racing, the most popular format of racing in the sport, as well as match racing. For those not convinced that good match racing would be possible in multihulls known for their lack of mobility (slow to tack) and for their instant acceleration in puffs that tends to separate the boats on the racecourse, the ACWS was revealing.

What made the ACWS successful was creative thinking backed by leading-edge technological innovation. America's Cup Race Management, in particular Regatta Director Iain Murray, with John Craig and Mike Martin, conceived the reaching start, novel course formats, vastly simplified racing rules, umpiring by race officials ashore,

Royal Swedish Yacht Club

and delineated course boundaries. All other sports have boundaries of some sort, but boundaries other than shallow water are a first in the history of yacht racing.

Stan Honey, director of technology for the America's Cup Event Authority, and his team were able to build AC LiveLine, the electronic system that gave life to the concepts. Honey, who brought us the yellow first-down line seen on televised NFL games, is a widely acclaimed racing sailor as well as an electrical engineering genius.

The boundaries he and his team created are electronic. Television viewers see them as a superimposed graphic on their screens. Crews are alerted to their boat's proximity to a boundary by a flashing yellow light. If they "hit" a boundary, they are penalized (electronically) by judges sitting at consoles ashore, watching televised feeds from helicopters, chase boats, and race boats.

Boundaries not only keep the fleet centered on the course, which facilitates close-quarter racing for television coverage,

but also add a key tactical element to the racing. Boats with right-of-way must allow boats coming off the boundary room to maneuver, a condition burdened boats can use to their advantage.

The boundaries, along with the rest of the stunning graphic ensemble Honey's team produced—colored wakes to identify boats; lay lines (which show the optimum course to a mark); start and finish lines; grids showing distances between boats; three boat-length circles around marks indicating penalty areas—constitute a package that has made sailing as television- and viewer-friendly as it has ever been.

At a stroke, a sport in which boats are powered by invisible forces, in which competitors make decisions based on what the layman can't see—a sport governed by a complex and arcane set of rules—became understandable to the viewer. Better still, the multihulls' significantly increased speeds across the entire wind range meant that races were not only shorter but could also be started reliably on time.

////////////

THE AC45S HAVE proved to be excellent trainers. Sailors love them. They are extremely fast and maneuverable, both tricky and rewarding to sail. Unlike the big multihulls of 2010 and the AC72s that followed, the AC45s have little instrumentation. Other than the AC LiveLine race management system, they require seat-of-the-pants sailing. Crews had to learn how to set up controls on the wing by feel and experience. And the boats proved surprisingly robust. Several of the AC45s capsized as sailors tested the edges of performance, and they were repaired and back on the water the following day.

The AC45s also opened the America's Cup to a new breed of sailor. For years, heavy monohull classes and the match

racing circuit have been predominant in funneling skippers into the America's Cup ranks. Now skippers are coming from high-speed, athletic dinghies like the 49er and a variety of multihulls, from A- and C-Class to ORMA 60s. Another big difference: These sailors are younger. They had better be. The AC45s and AC72s are not your father's America's Cup yachts. What bronco busting is to rodeo, racing AC45s is to sailing. The crews are built like NFL linebackers and just as fit. Until 2010, the average age of a Cup skipper was thirty-eight. A quick poll of the America's Cup World Series skippers reduced that average by several years. The youngest among them was twenty-one.

////////////

» **OPPOSITE** Luna Rossa Challenge during an early AC72 training session off Auckland, New Zealand.
» **BELOW** AC LiveLine allows television viewers to see course boundaries, boat speed, and penalties.
» **BOTTOM** An early AC45 in build at Core Builders Composites in New Zealand.

The advent of 72-foot multihulls with fixed wings has made a crew's need to reduce power before crossing the line a do or crash-and-burn proposition.

MOVING FROM THE AC45s to the 72s was a significant leap for all the teams. One of the most impressive first looks at the AC72 was a video released by Emirates Team New Zealand that showed its boat hitting 35 knots. A chase boat, with four 300 horsepower outboards lashed to the transom at full crank, was struggling to keep up. At that speed, for a long, impossible moment, the AC72's dagger foils lifted both hulls out of the water. The 72-foot, 13,000-pound catamaran under wing power was foiling. Seeing was believing.

Like the multihull behemoths from 2010 that helped orchestrate this sea change in the America's Cup, the AC72s are technological marvels. Hundreds of electronic strain gauges have been molded into the hulls and wings. All have readouts to help crews avoid what is called in auto racing "hitting the wall." Just as a driver's race is over after his car goes into the wall, if a crew capsizes an AC72 during a Cup race, there will be no tomorrow. Witness the extensive wing damage done when ORACLE TEAM USA's AC72 capsized while practicing in 25 knots of wind in October 2012. In a multihull, the maximum performance is outside the limit of what the boat can withstand. Therefore, crews in the 34th America's Cup finals must constantly recalibrate where they feel the edge is and how far they are prepared to go beyond it in order to win.

Reducing sail, throttling back, has always been a part of sailing in the interest of obtaining maximum boatspeed and control in strong winds. In offshore races, prudent skippers throttle back to avoid losing a mast. But the advent of 72-foot multihulls with fixed wings has made a crew's need to reduce power before crossing the line a do or crash-and-burn proposition. As we have seen, make a mistake, and it's over in the blink of an eye. ◆

SETTING THE SCENE:
SAN

FRANCISCO

For a walk on the wild side, the America's Cup had to come to the Wild West. For the ethos. For the physicality. For the hint of an oceanic wilderness that slips in on the sea breeze to haunt even the haughtiest of San Francisco's penthouse parlors.

There is a San Francisco way of being, and it has its source in the origins of the city itself, sprung up almost overnight in the Gold Rush and reinvented again and again over a century and a half by successive waves of migration and social movements. It has something to do with the city heights, heights that make for inner-city views of the sea and open parkland, elbow room stretching up the coastline to Point Reyes. The very words "the hills of San Francisco" have music in them.

The San Francisco way of being never feels shut in. It's about the waters, surrounding, defining the peninsula in a constant reminder that this was a city built from the sea. The early Miwoks and Ohlones traveled by reed boat. The first Europeans arrived under sail, followed by ships laden with shovels and pickaxes, bullets and lace, schoolmarms by the dozens and fancy ladies by the thousands and, by and by, the accoutrement of culture. San Francisco is a young city, but it has history.

Beneath the America's Cup Park at Pier 27—soon to become the city's new cruise ship terminal—lie the hulks of sailing ships that braved Cape Horn in 1849. They lie where they were abandoned in the fever for quick riches. Now the Cup provides an opportunity to speed the reinvention of a once-thriving waterfront that went to seed a generation ago when the Northern California shipping industry converted to container shipping and moved to Oakland. Having the Cup as the first tenant of the new terminal building is just one mark of a revitalization that can

The San Francisco climate is unique and counterintuitive.

be seen from Fisherman's Wharf all the way to the base camp of ORACLE TEAM USA, near the opposite end of the port.

America's Cup defender Larry Ellison, the man behind ORACLE TEAM USA, made his billions as a techie. He doesn't write code anymore—he has people for that. But Ellison fronted the development of brilliant new sports graphics for the 2013 Cup, a system so precise and encompassing that the race committee uses it to lay the course and the umpires use it to make calls. Ellison also backed the open-source initiative that feeds racing data to any hacker who wants to play. The San Francisco America's Cup is *the* technology Cup (it would not be possible to even imagine an AC72 designed with a slide rule) happening in the city's own high-tech moment and movement. SOMA, the South of Market Area, buzzes with start-ups and twenty-something coders with deep pockets. It may be the south side of town, but SOMA's new condo towers soar, looking above and beyond the fabled hills of San Francisco all the way to the racecourse of America's Cup 2013.

» **PAGES 24–25** Luna Rossa, Team Korea, and ORACLE TEAM USA run toward a cheering crowd and remarkable skyline in San Francisco. » **ABOVE** The Bay Bridge and San Francisco skyline as seen on a clear evening from Treasure Island. » **BELOW** The "Forest of Masts" panorama illustrates the innumerable boats abandoned in the San Francisco Bay during the Gold Rush and acts as a reminder that the city was built from the sea.

» AC45 fleet moored in Marina Harbor, San Francisco. The city is known for its perennial fog but also delivers spectacular sunsets.

» **BELOW** Victorian homes line San Francisco's panhandle. » **BOTTOM** Though a popular tourist destination, there are still plenty of in-service, hard-working fisherman and crabbing boats docked at Hyde Street Pier, in Fisherman's Wharf.

Once upon a time in this town, "living on the edge" meant the Grateful Dead playing for free in the Golden Gate Park Panhandle with Victorian gingerbread houses all around. The city has moved on, but the Dead live on, and the beat goes on. San Francisco has always been a crazy quilt of contrasts. Even natives can take a minivacation just by touring across town, and the climate will probably be different when they get there.

Thanks to the sea breeze that attracted the America's Cup to the bay, San Franciscans breathe the freshest urban air on the planet. Depending on their exposure to that same ocean-chilled breeze, families just blocks apart can live in radically different microclimates. The art-hip, mural-rich Mission District, in the shelter of the city's highest hill, is

the sunniest and warmest of the city's neighborhoods. And yes, we *are* talking summer weather, something surprisingly elusive for a city in sunny California. The San Francisco climate is unique and counterintuitive. Those in the know dress in layers. The sea breeze cranks and the chill bites—even in July—but atop any hill, looking out across a white-capped bay to parkland and mountains over yonder, there is never a feeling of being trapped in the city.

Locals tend to shun Fisherman's Wharf, but those who haven't been there must go. In truth, there are good eats and historic ships. Ogle the old timers of the San Francisco Maritime National Historic Park for free, but don't overlook the in-service, steam-powered Liberty Ship and the diesel submarine down the way.

Pacific Heights and the Haight-Ashbury are pocketed with Victorian houses, trim, colorful, and replete with story and scandal. It's that kind of town. From the Haight to the high-end shopping of Union Square is a long walk, but it's a short walk from there to the bustle of old Chinatown, where shop windows offer baubles for the tourists, row upon row of poultry strung up for the locals, and teas and acupuncture for whatever ails. Back in the day, tour guides would lead the way into the back rooms of such establishments to show off "an authentic opium den" and throw in some excitement by staging (and escaping) a fake police raid.

Cross one street and suddenly you're in North Beach, still oozing Italian heritage. City Lights Booksellers and Publishers, co-founded by poet Lawrence Ferlinghetti, harkens to the Beats of the 1950s and is still a force today. So is Francis Ford Coppola's American Zoetrope studio, occupying the copper-green flatiron Sentinel Building that anchors the view toward the Transamerica Pyramid. There are coffee houses and bars enough to get anyone through the day or night. Yes, that could be Bono, the rocker, having one at Tosca. Yes, there's a table at the Caffe Trieste that was Bill Cosby's choice when he was doing standup at the hungry i.

You could take in any or several of these neighborhoods in an hour or relish the details of just one. An hour's drive (longer, on a crowded summer weekend) could get you to the wine country, or the beginnings of the redwood forest, or a coastline of pounding surf and tiny hamlets. It's all so near and yet so far from the pulse of the city.

Twenty-eight museums make San Francisco a museum town, too. Along

with the standard bearers, SFMOMA in downtown and the de Young in Golden Gate Park, there are the very special sleepers. The Legion of Honor is a gem on a hilltop overlooking the blustery Golden Gate Strait. The Walt Disney Family Museum is tucked into a former U.S. Army barracks along the parade ground of the Presidio, a uniquely urban national park. There's the Exploratorium, a hands-on science experience for all ages in the Marina, and the California Academy of Sciences just steps from the de Young.

San Francisco is a town for walking and discovering. Anyone can tell you that Noe Valley vaunts charming boutiques, that the Castro throws a mean parade, or that the Mission has a thriving arts scene and a hopping Latin style, but even most natives haven't yet discovered its cluster of artisan ice cream shops. In San Francisco, there is always something old and something new. The America's Cup is old to the world, new to San Francisco; but just as Sweden, Italy, and New Zealand are looking to take it away, the locals are hoping to see the Cup stick around for a long, long time. ♦

» **TOP** Every time there is an America's Cup match, the winner is inscribed on the silver trophy. » **ABOVE** San Francisco's China Town is the largest and most densely populated outside Asia.

» Once the site of a lookout that would signal the nature of incoming boats, today Telegraph Hill is punctuated by Coit Tower.

THE GOLDEN GATE BRIDGE

WHETHER IT BE a glimpse of its fire-toned towers from afar, a stroll over its blustery, near-9,000-foot span, or a float from the bay to the Pacific beneath its sublime shadows, it takes only one encounter with the Golden Gate Bridge to understand its powerful hold on the imagination. Effortlessly iconic, the bridge is a tribute to human artistry without flaunting it, reaching across the Golden Gate Strait so naturally that one feels as if it has always been there to connect travelers, greet seafarers, and see them off.

It's almost surprising to learn that, on May 27, 2012, the bridge celebrated its seventy-fifth anniversary. It is timeless, and has aged well, if at all, since the 1930s, when it was a symbol for economic prosperity and a beacon to motorists in the early age of the automobile. Today the Golden Gate Bridge is a powerful source of identity for the Bay Area. Successful in promoting prosperity and growth in Northern California when first constructed, today it supports the region as a cornerstone of the area's public transportation infrastructure and serves as a powerful attraction for thousands of tourists and sightseers who visit the city on an annual basis. Erected during the era of optimism, cooperation, and hope, today the bridge remains a symbol of an almost utopian sense of community as well as a source of pride for residents of the Bay Area.

When you enter the roadway of the bridge from the Marin side, you are immediately struck by a feeling of expansiveness, as if space and time were opening up and each tower was a portal into another world. This feeling, along with the impressive views of San Francisco and the vastness of the Pacific Ocean, have made the bridge the best example of the San Francisco tradition of using science and human ingenuity to alter the land while also showing reverence for it. No one can say that the Golden Gate Bridge is a structure that mars the natural beauty that surrounds it. Rather, this triumph of design and engineering enhances the landscape it belongs to. And in this sense it is like the materialization of a dream—a true marvel.

—Peter Beren, author of *The Golden Gate*

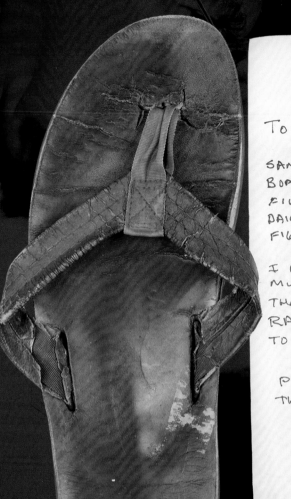

Mileage Plus...

BRINGING THE

CUP

TO THE

BAY

IN 1987, TOM BLACKALLER prophesied: "If
we ever get the America's Cup to San Francisco
Bay, we'll show the world how good sailing can
be." Blackaller was the bay's sailing hero of his
generation, an America's Cup contender, and a
catamaran sailor to boot. He was a man who could imagine (not that he
believed it would really happen) Cup competition in cats. Twice he had skippered boats hoping to defend the Cup for the New York Yacht Club, losing
the defender trials each time to Dennis Conner. His second attempt was
in 1983, the year that Conner went on to lose the Cup to Australia after 132
years of U.S. domination. In this "friendly competition between foreign
countries," that event opened the door for Blackaller to challenge to win the
Cup back for the United States, not on behalf of the New York Yacht Club, but
for his home base on the San Francisco city front, St. Francis Yacht Club.

Blackaller went to Australia in 1987 with a radical boat carrying fore and aft foils (a.k.a. rudders) to keep the boat from slipping sideways instead of the usual long keel. Replacing the keel was a thin, deep strut with a lead ballast bulb at the bottom. The boat showed bursts of unbeatable speed, but the complexities of the bow rudder–stern rudder interaction were not resolved soon enough. Naval architects would later reinterpret the concept to create record-setting ocean racers, but too late for that first attempt to bring the Cup to San Francisco Bay.

Instead, Dennis Conner won in 1987 and took the Cup to the San Diego Yacht Club, where SF Bay sailors remained

deeply involved. Native son Paul Cayard, Blackaller's backup skipper and tactician in 1987, skippered Italy's challenger, *Il Moro di Venezia*, in 1992 and helmed the slow-as-Christmas U.S. defender in 1995 against a triumphant New Zealand. Meanwhile, round-the-world-race veteran Dawn Riley crewed the winning *America³* in 1992 and served as team captain in 1995.

For the Kiwis' first defense, in 2000, not one but two SF Bay challenges arose. Cayard led *AmericaOne* under the colors of St. Francis Yacht Club, with John Kostecki as tactician—yes, the same "JK" who was tactician for ORACLE's winning effort in 2010, continuing with the team through the switch to catamarans. The San Francisco Yacht Club—the oldest yacht club on the West Coast, founded in 1869—fielded a challenge led by Dawn Riley. Both teams made the Louis Vuitton Cup semifinals. *America-One* made the finals but lost the shoot-out to Luna Rossa, an outcome that turned largely upon the failures of a

ANSWERING AN EARLY INVITATION TO SAN FRANCISCO BAY

Not surprisingly, San Francisco has been championed as the ideal venue to host the America's Cup for more than a century. In 1903, Rufus P. Jennings and the California Promotion Committee sent a letter to C. Oliver Iselin, the managing partner of *Reliance*, suggesting that it could offer near perfect conditions in San Francisco Bay. With strong, reliable winds from June to August, the landlocked harbor could ensure "a safe and exciting contest which could be viewed from beginning to end by spectators upon the land." However, the New York Yacht Club was the holder of the America's Cup, and it would have been unthinkable for the club to schedule racing anywhere but at its own regatta site. It would be 110 years before the invitation was finally accepted and its claims put to the test.

» **LEFT** Ernesto Betarelli hoists the America's Cup trophy after team Alinghi's successful defense in Valencia, Spain.
» **ABOVE** After years of legal disputes, BMW ORACLE Racing challenged for and won the America's Cup in 2010, bringing the trophy to San Francisco.

certain run of green spinnaker cloth. To this day, there are locals who shiver at the sight of that shade of green.

Longtime sailor Larry Ellison bought the assets of *AmericaOne* and then, with new boats, competed in New Zealand in 2003. The Cup left New Zealand that year, but his BMW ORACLE team then became the Challenger of Record for the 32nd America's Cup in Valencia, Spain. There were an unprecedented ten teams challenging the defender, Alinghi—but only a few were actually a threat.

What went wrong after a splendid regatta in 2007 is not to be told here, but things went very wrong immediately after Alinghi's successful defense. From July 2007 to February 2010 every Cup conversation was about legal disputes, leading to a court-dictated match between the defender, Team Alinghi's giant catamaran, and the court-recognized challenger, BMW ORACLE's giant trimaran—a beast with a solid wing too tall to fit under the Golden Gate Bridge. On February 14, off the Mediterranean coast of Spain—in the greatest Valentine's Day gift imaginable—ORACLE's *USA-17* crossed the line a winner. The America's Cup suddenly belonged to San Francisco Bay. ♦

» ORACLE TEAM USA on San Francisco Bay. In addition to speed, camera- and spectator-friendly backdrops are central to the 34th America's Cup.

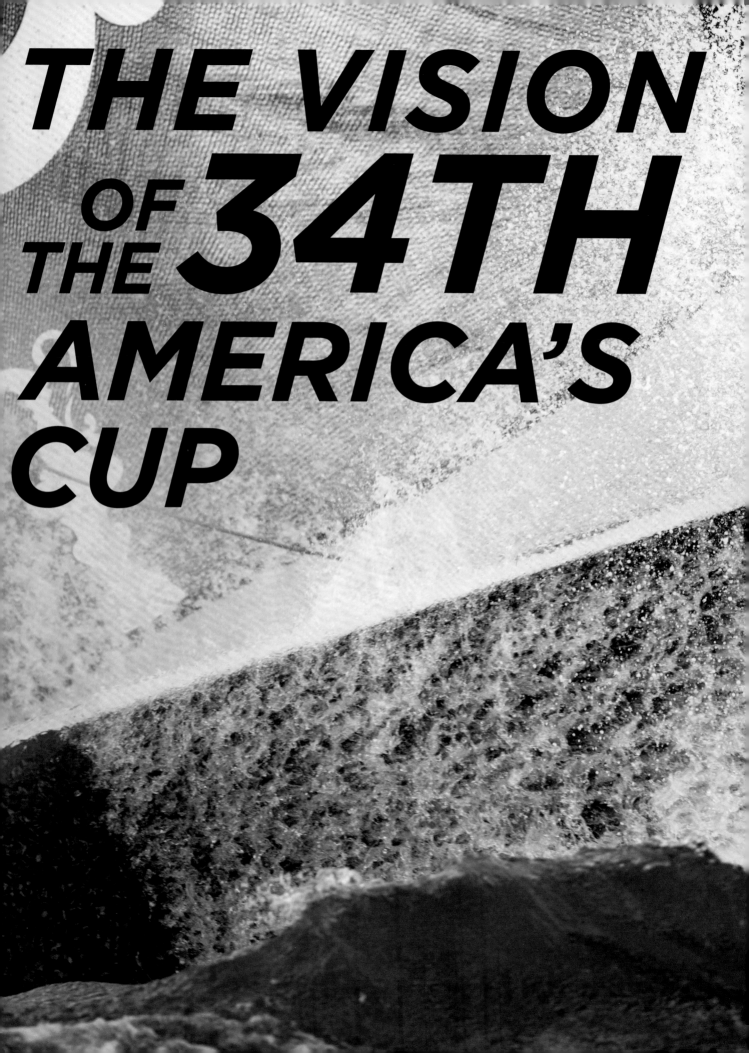

THE VISION OF THE **34TH** AMERICA'S CUP

» **PAGES 44-45** Energy Team dealing with the elements during an America's Cup World Series regatta in San Francisco. » **ABOVE** San Francisco Mayor Ed Lee (right) welcomes ORACLE TEAM USA CEO Russell Coutts during the signing of the agreement to host the America's Cup in San Francisco.

When Larry Ellison's BMW ORACLE Racing team beat Alinghi to win the 33rd America's Cup in 2010, it was immediately clear that a new era in the America's Cup had started.

Each time the trophy has moved to a new country with a new winner, the competition has evolved, but this would be on another scale. This would be dramatic change driven by a vision of creating an America's Cup for the twenty-first century.

The America's Cup has changed in the past, but never has it made a leap like this. New boats have been used before, but the AC72s, nicknamed "the beast" and "man-eater," are a broad and unprecedented step forward. The race format and rules have changed, too, but never to such dramatic effect. The way the story of the racing is told has always evolved with the times, but AC LiveLine, the technology behind the new America's Cup television broadcasts, is more than an evolution; it has changed the sport.

Although both monohulls and multihulls were considered for the new America's Cup Class, it soon became clear that the multihull offered several critical advantages. The power-to-weight ratio of the new design would ensure eye-popping speeds. With little draft requirements, the boats could race inshore, close to spectators, providing a "stadium sailing" experience never before seen in the America's Cup. And the new design would challenge the crews physically beyond anything they'd ever experienced. When asked about the demands inherent in designing the AC72s and sailing them in a fast-paced, close-quarters format, Russell Coutts explained, "It's the America's Cup; it's not supposed to be easy."

Could Lawrence Joseph Ellison have imagined any of this when he was just one more student at the University of California, Berkeley, one more left brain learning coding, one more starry-eyed kid rigging a boat at everybody's favorite sweat-equity outfit, the Cal Sailing Club, and gazing out to San Francisco Bay? The lure was powerful, and we have to respect the sense of adventure that drew him along on the day that he truly discovered San Francisco Bay.

Cal Sailing offered Lido 14s in those days, hardy little 14-footers capable of surviving conditions well beyond their intended use. That was a good thing. Let's picture our doughty craft and its lone sailor clearing the Berkeley shore with all of San Francisco Bay opening to the west, 9.9 miles to the Golden Gate Bridge, 3,749 boatlengths in a Lido 14. As the day goes along, the breeze builds. This is the ordinary pattern in the sailing season here, and we are speaking of a journey that takes hours, plenty of time for the day to "develop." Beyond the halfway mark lies Alcatraz, once home but hardly homey to Al Capone, now a windswept mishmash of restored prison structures, decaying prison structures, and guano-coated rock. At this point, the breeze is stiff but manageable, and the combination of seascape and

» **RIGHT** Larry Ellison on board one of ORACLE TEAM USA's AC45s during a training session in San Francisco. » **BELOW** Emirates Team New Zealand and Luna Rossa Challenge show San Francisco spectators how exciting match racing in catamarans can be during an America's Cup World Series regatta in San Francisco.

landscape is dotted with iconic images. On one hand, there is the skyline of the city, and on the other, mountains rising away to the north. But the lodestone pulling us forward is that bright-red bridge that spans the entrance to San Francisco Bay, spanning also the passage to the vastness of the sea. For a sailor, it is fascination pure and simple to sail under that bridge. You have to do it. You just have to.

And the moment stays with you forever. The roar of traffic two hundred feet overhead. The rattle of wheels on the roadway. The startling shadow as you pass beneath. The howl of the breeze as it picks up. The sudden change in the world around you.

➤

Let's be clear. The Golden Gate Strait, seaward of the bridge, is not always a howling maelstrom. But often enough, it is exactly that, and Lawrence Joseph Ellison, just plain Larry to his friends at Cal, had blundered into one of those often enough. Call it a learning experience. The steep, white-capped waves breaking over the bow were too much for his little boat, and just finding a moment to turn—being broadside is the ugliest moment, the worst exposure—

was an act of art, science, and dire hope. We know he made it, of course. In the process, he also made a bargain: "I said, if God will just let me make it back under that bridge, safe in San Francisco Bay, I will never do this again." And he didn't. But he also did not give up that part of himself that will boldly embark upon the unmarked path.

➤

Ellison set out years ago to win the America's Cup by conventional means, little imagining the strange road he would travel. His appetite had been whetted by winning four Maxi Class world championships with his 80-foot ocean racer, *Sayonara*. However, the famously brutal, stormy 1998 Sydney-Hobart Race in that boat had killed his appetite for competing long distance on the ocean. Of 115 boats that started Australia's Blue Water Classic that year, only 44 completed the 630-mile course, five boats sank, and six lives were lost.

Ellison was ready for a new challenge, and he launched out by purchasing the assets of Paul Cayard's *AmericaOne* campaign at the conclusion of the 2000 races in Auckland. By 2010, flying the colors of the Golden Gate Yacht Club, he had fought through

conventional Cup cycles in 2003 and 2007 and won the rancorous Deed of Gift match that brought the Cup to San Francisco. Along the way, he and Russell Coutts confirmed their conviction that Cup competition, as the inevitable apex of big-boat racing, needed a new direction. Every attempt to create an alternative had failed. Only the America's Cup could be the America's Cup, but it had outgrown its original, nineteenth-century concept and could not escape what it had become—an antique competition lingering in a modern era, eating its face off.

Over time, the teams and the racing had grown fully professionalized, but without a business model. Relative to their skill sets and relative to other sports, the sailors were underpaid. And although various sponsors used the team bases and action on the water as opportunities for relationship marketing, offsetting some costs, an America's Cup team was nothing like a baseball team, where success could turn a profit. It didn't take a genius to recognize that even baseball does not survive on ticket sales. It's about television.

In 2007, Russell Coutts and Paul Cayard teamed up to promote an international circuit in 80-foot catamarans. That was one more grand scheme that never got off the ground, one could argue, because it lacked that certain element rooted as much in hard-nosed reality as in the cliché that expresses it, the Holy Grail of sailing, the America's Cup. Then came 2010. Up to the moment of winning the Cup, all the focus, all the energy in Ellison's racing team had been directed toward the race. After a break to absorb that they really had succeeded, and against tremendous odds, the new defenders began to reimagine the America's Cup, bottom to top.

Ellison and Coutts looked to the long term, with a mind to leave a legacy of a business-based America's Cup that would be better for the competitors and better for the sport, drawing on an all-new fan base of sports lovers from outside the world of sailing. They were swimming against history, and traditionalists were apoplectic. But, by and by, the traditionalists who actually witnessed the "new deal," whether on the waterfront or on television, became converts. It was the boats on the water—first the AC45s then the staggering AC72s—that opened minds. ♦

AC LIVELINE
BECOMES THE PIPELINE

WHEN LARRY ELLISON'S TEAM WON the 33rd America's Cup, Ellison was clear that for sailing to grow, it had to get its television right. He was equally clear that the transformation would require more cameras, better cameras, audio feeds, and, most of all, a revolution in sports graphics, visual aids to help anyone, even non-sailors, understand the action. He told an interviewer, "When the NFL put that yellow first-down line on the field, it gave the fan a little more insight. The guy who did the yellow line is named Stan Honey. I've sailed with him." That was the spark.

One of the great sailors of his generation and arguably the greatest ocean navigator, Stan Honey is also a software developer and entrepreneur. In the 1980s, during his early career at the Stanford Research Institute, he developed over-the-horizon radar systems for the military.

When the NFL put that yellow first-down line on the field, it gave the fan a little more insight.

He also built one of the first onboard computers for an ocean racing boat, incorporating velocity-made-good monitoring and position fixing. New code was written, components were fabricated for specific purposes, and a successful Transpacific Yacht Race inspired Honey and the boat's owner, Nolan Bushnell, to team up to create Etak, builder of the original in-vehicle navigation system.

Later, Honey and his Stanford Research Institute colleague Ken Milnes would co-found a sports-graphics company, Sportvision, source of the yellow line in football and strike-zone tracking in baseball. Both technologies

won Emmys. Then came illuminated hockey pucks, car tracking in NASCAR, and Honey's 2010 round-the-world record attempt on a 105-foot trimaran, *Groupama 3*, with Honey being the only non-French sailor in the crew (which tells you something about his international standing). The ice-dodging, spray-flying record attempt would succeed—28,000 miles at an average speed of 24.6 knots, fast enough to pull a water-skier. Somewhere beyond the halfway point, braced in front of his array of instruments in *Groupama 3*'s navigation station, Honey would receive an email from his wife, Sally, a two-time U.S. Yachtswoman of the Year. An interview transcript was attached. It was the interview in which Larry Ellison was explaining his vision of how to make sailing easier to understand on television. He was talking about the yellow line in football and how he had sailed with the man who created it. Honey had navigated Ellison's champion Maxi, *Sayonara*. The two had not kept up in the years since. "But I sat there," Honey would recall, "and I thought to myself, *I guess I know what I'm going to be doing next.*"

Honey had been long aware that the technology was available to reinvent sailing on TV. The budget had been lacking, and the will. But the 2010 U.S. Sailor of the Year (inducted into the National Sailing Hall of Fame in 2012) now had the green light to recruit his former business partners, Milnes and Tim Heidemann, and launch a shoot-the-moon agenda. The mission now was to bring the advantages of CG to the live broadcast—to display wind direction, current differentials, and imaginary right-of-way lines right on the water, in the middle of the action, whenever the commentators needed them to help tell the story.

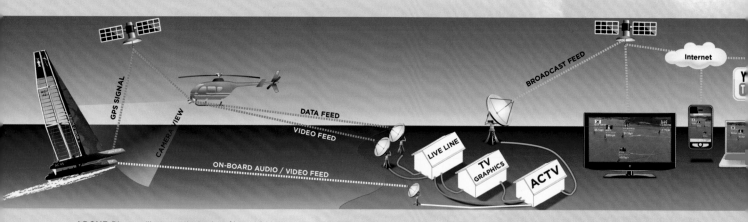

» ABOVE Diagram illustrates the basics of how AC LiveLine brings race data from the water to home televisions and mobile devices. **» OPPOSITE TOP** The America's Cup World Series television compound at Cascais, where technicians could view onboard video and AC LiveLine data. **» OPPOSITE BOTTOM** The visual package delivered by AC LiveLine allows even expert sailors to comprehend much more than they could with the naked eye.

Thinking closely about that yellow line in football, there is the obvious problem of not "painting" over the players and the referees. To that technological challenge, add that a football field is not flat but mounded (for runoff), and the software must make corrections from multiple angles to create the illusion of a yellow line perfectly parallel to the chalk lines on the mounded field. Then add the requirement to correct simultaneously for the distortion in a television lens. Don't forget to add inertial sensors to correct for those college games, where the cameras are mounted on the stands, which get to rockin' when the kids do.

But that is easy compared to taking the AC LiveLine bundle of technologies out of the relatively controlled, fixed world, moving it to the harsh environment of salt water,

boats, and helicopters, and painting electronic lines on the water with a positioning tolerance of only 2 centimeters. Then consider the complexities of writing integrated code to correct simultaneously for the curvature of the Earth. No one expected immediate perfection, but early glitches and all, the system the sailors call "Stanware" clicked into place so quickly and with such precision that, suddenly, the Race Committee and the umpires wanted to use it, too.

With its 2-centimeter tolerance, AC LiveLine can catch a boat that makes a premature start, and the Race Committee can penalize it with confidence. Even with the much slower boats of old, eyeballs could make mistakes. With AC72s moving at startling speeds, the eyeball would be too twentieth century.

Umpires, accustomed to chasing the racers in motorboats, now had tools that removed the judgment from their calls and eliminated guesswork that once seemed inevitable. For example, there is an imaginary circle around each turning mark, and that circle can be critical. The first boat to enter it gains the right-of-way for rounding and probably gains the lead on the next leg. But you won't be surprised to hear that, in the past, sailors and even umpires often disagreed as to the position of an imaginary circle on the water. The new electronics package removes the guesswork.

In 2013, the entire racecourse is dynamic, managed electronically, with Principal Race Officer John Craig adjusting the length of each race—longer or shorter—to suit an assigned schedule. Instead of buoys tethered to anchors, marks are boats with geopositioning capability that stay in one spot, or move, according to the master plan. Course boundaries and protest and penalty communications are all integrated into a package of software and hardware that at this point is too expensive and complex for ordinary sailing contests.

The America's Cup has a long tradition of technological trickle down, however. It will take a few years, but key elements of the package will eventually find their way to other high-end racecourses. What began as a determination to make sailing understandable on TV has gone beyond. The proof of concept is the human reaction to what Honey likes to call "augmented reality." There are cameras in the air and on the boats. The sailors are wired for sound, and for the first time they are forbidden to turn off their mics. Technology makes it crystal clear who is ahead and who is behind. It is now perfectly normal for people at the races to watch the race as the boats come near. And then, as the boats speed away, spray flying, the audience turns to study the race on TV or a tablet, where even an expert sailor can see and comprehend so much more.

THE
AMERICA'S CUP
WORLD SERIES

An all-multihull competition that wasn't a result of a court ruling represented a first in the event's history. The aim of the America's Cup World Series—and the brand-new one-design wing sail-powered AC45 catamarans competing in it—was to help fast-track the teams' understanding of these radical new state-of-the-art craft and to create a circuit that would showcase the incredible speed, the tight course layouts, and the spectacle central to the revolutionizing vision of the 34th America's Cup.

For the organizers, the new circuit provided the opportunity to develop every aspect of the competition prior to its incorporation into the America's Cup proper, including the creation of the best "made for television" yacht-racing event. Iain Murray, the dynamic regatta director and CEO of America's Cup Race Management, was ideally positioned to do this. Not only did he have a history of skippering yachts in past America's Cups, but he was also instrumental in getting the high-performance 18-foot skiff racing on Sydney Harbour onto prime-time television in Australia in the 1980s.

Creating the AC45s proved a monumental task. The boat was drawn up by ORACLE TEAM USA's in-house designers. It was then constructed by their elite boatbuilding team, Core Builders Composites, led by Tim Smyth and Mark Turner and operating out of a new facility set up for the purpose in Warkworth, New Zealand. Incredibly, with the help of many subcontractors from the New Zealand boating and composites industries, design to launch took just five months.

In August 2011, just six months after the launch of the first AC45, the whole sailing world and the America's Cup community looked on as nine AC45s lined up for the first America's Cup World Series regatta in Cascais, Portugal.

═══

Combining match racing with full fleet racing and speed trials, the regatta in Cascais was unlike anything seen before in sailing. This was the first time that a group of yachts as large as 45 feet and fitted with giant vertical airplane-wing-type rigs had ever raced en masse. Anticipation among the spectators and viewers from around the world was as great as the trepidation among the fledgling crews.

Sailing the boats were many old hands from past America's Cups, highly experienced sailors such as Terry Hutchinson, Ray Davies, and Paul Cayard, who had to go back to school to get to grips with the high-octane new boats and their towering unfamiliar rigs. To help accelerate their learning, most of the teams brought in

» **PAGES 52-53** America's Cup World Series boats line up for a reaching start during a fleet regatta in San Francisco.
» **LEFT** The AC45s took serious abuse throughout the America's Cup World Series, making plenty of work for onshore crew who developed a keen eye for detail. » **BELOW** Emirates Team New Zealand streaking downwind on San Francisco Bay.

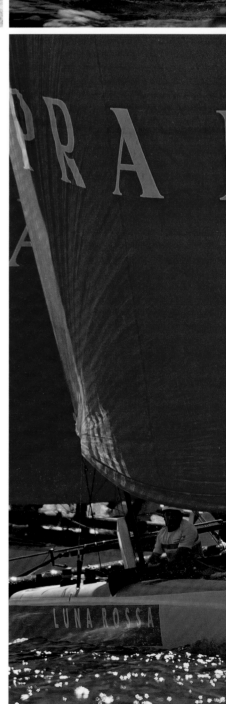

» **TOP LEFT** ORACLE TEAM USA Spithill. » **TOP CENTER** Energy Team's Devan Le Bihan hiking out.
» **TOP RIGHT** Luna Rossa Piranha (front) and Luna Rossa Swordfish neck and neck in San Francisco.
» **RIGHT** Luna Rossa Swordfish (left) and ORACLE TEAM USA (right) in Cascais. Even in mild conditions,
the AC45s offered spectacular racing.

catamaran specialists from the Olympic Games or the Extreme Sailing Series. Even
among the more seasoned multihull sailors, only Jimmy Spithill's ORACLE TEAM
USA crew had ever raced with a wing sail before. As skipper Chris Draper put it—the
wing sails were "a great leveler" between the teams.

Even the sound of the regatta was different—no flogging mainsails, no spinnaker
drops, just the silent power and efficiency of the wing and the furling headsails and the
hiss of lightweight carbon-fiber hulls skimming across the top of the water.

As the America's Cup World Series went on tour—visiting first Plymouth, England,
and San Diego, California, then in 2012 on to Naples and Venice in Italy and back to the
United States with events in Newport, Rhode Island, and San Francisco—the racing
format also progressed. For regular sailing fans, this came as another eye-opener.

Iain Murray and his race management team had come up with a new course
format. Usually inshore yacht races are "windward-leeward": zigzagging into the
wind and rounding a weather mark before heading back downwind. The new format
involved a "reaching start," across the wind on the AC45's fastest point of sail on a
short initial leg to a first mark. The twin-hulled speedsters would hurtle into this
mark in unison, with all the drama of the first corner in a Formula One race. Traditionally, America's Cup racing was a defensive game, with the early leader trying the
block and parry for the rest of the race. Now it was an attacking game, the reaching
start producing overtaking opportunities straight off the start line.

For the AC45 crews, the game involved jockeying to find a position on the start
line: Who could best "pull the trigger," accelerating out of the start the fastest, and
then who was the most fearless rounding the first mark in the optimum position
without causing a collision.

There was also a new element of physicality. Russell Coutts had promised that
the AC45s would provide a thorough workout for the crews. With just five sailors
on board, the boats were short staffed. Another new feature of the racing that made
them work all the harder.

Although sailing is traditionally a slow sport, AC45 competition is just the opposite—as fast and intense as it comes, even in light winds. The ability of the AC45s to provide riveting racing even in mild conditions was immediately put to the test at the first ACWS event in Cascais. Although conventional yacht racing in such conditions would have been dull for spectators, the speedy catamarans were fully powered up in as little at 7 knots of wind.

Seeing a fleet of eleven boats (the fleet grew from nine to eleven over the course of the first season) screaming out of the start line and piling into the first reaching mark was the most exciting moment in all of televised sailing. Around the racecourse, the action came thick and fast, with crews unable to catch their breath before they reached a course boundary and were forced to tack or jibe. The crews were a blur of constant activity—trimming the sails or the wing, raising and lowering the daggerboard, tacking or jibing sails during maneuvers, and dropping and hoisting sails at mark roundings. And in big conditions, this all occurs as they are being dowsed in spray flying back from the bow with the force of a fire hydrant.

In addition to all of this, the competitive nature of the ACWS was severe—unlike the AC72s to come, all the AC45s were identical, and teams had little opportunity to gain any technical advantage. As Mark Bulkeley, crewman on Team Korea, put it, "Almost everyone can win races and hold good spots, so it means that it is just full-on. It is really hard to pull away and it is so easy to get sucked back in. You can be in third and you can get one tiny shift wrong and suddenly you are seventh, back in this group of six or seven boats that are fighting each other."

The ACWS may have been conceived as training ground for both the sailors and the America's Cup Event Authority, but it also proved to be a remarkable test of endurance for both the sailors and their AC45s, and a remarkable display of the new-style America's Cup racing—a million miles from the heavyweight monohulls of the past lumbering out to one side or another of a giant triangle somewhere well away from land. ♦

The Louis Vuitton Cup
THE AMERICA'S CUP CHALLENGER SERIES

WHEN THE AMERICA'S CUP summer of 1983 began off Newport, Rhode Island, no challenger had ever won the America's Cup. Then along came the Louis Vuitton Cup, which did for America's Cup challengers what had never been done before by giving them a structured series of competition where they could hone their skills and improve their chances of victory against the American defender.

Australia II, headed by Alan Bond and John Bertrand, won the inaugural Louis Vuitton Cup in 1983, and then went on to win the America's Cup, ending the New York Yacht Club's 132-year winning streak. Nearly four years later a similar story played out when Dennis Conner's Stars & Stripes won the Louis Vuitton Cup and then the America's Cup, returning the trophy to American soil.

The back-to-back victories by a challenger after 132 years of defender dominance spawned the brilliant slogan: To win the America's Cup, first win the Louis Vuitton Cup. The summer of 2013 marks the 30-year anniversary of the Louis Vuitton Cup, and the phrase is alive and well.

»ABOVE Prada during the 2000 Louis Vuitton Cup in New Zealand.

THE VINTAGE ESTATE
YOUNTVILLE

Park Your Car.
Escape on Foot.

For those who crave escape within strolling distance of your hotel, The Vintage Estate *is* that incomparable destination in the epicurean walking town of Yountville, offering Napa Valley's most exceptional experiences at your doorstep. Just a leisurely saunter from your guestroom, you'll find yourself indulging in the nation's *per capita* Michelin Star capital of dining, premier wine tasting rooms, intimate spa experiences, lifestyle shopping, romantic art, history and culture of the country's most lauded wine region without so much as the turn of a car key.

For pleasure, for business, and affordable luxury at its finest, visit our website and make your escape today...

www.vintageestate.com

V Marketplace
Open 10am - 5:30pm Daily
707.944.2451 / www.vmarketplace.com

Reservations
800.351.1133
www.vintageinn.com

Group Sales
Corporate & Social Events
707.945.4545 / www.villagio.com

6481 Washington Street ▪ Yountville, California 94599

ARTEMIS RACING

THE CHALLENGER OF RECORD

TORBJÖRN TÖRNQVIST made a rapid ascent from his start in sailing. Beginning in 2005, his combination of leadership skills and strategic acumen led Artemis Racing to championships in the hard-fought TP52 and RC44 fleets and inspired the team's confidence to challenge for the America's Cup. Soon after the America's Cup arrived in San Francisco, Törnqvist made the announcement that he would challenge on behalf of KSSS, Kungliga Svenska Segel Sällskapet, an institution founded in 1830. In English, it's the Royal Swedish Yacht Club, and today it has five thousand members across Sweden.

» Artemis Racing CEO Paul Cayard assesses the team's AC72 during an early training session on San Francisco Bay.

» TOP Like ORACLE TEAM USA, Artemis Racing opted to remain in the Bay Area for winter training rather than move their operation to New Zealand. **» ABOVE** Artemis Racing helmsman Nathan Outteridge. **» OPPOSITE TOP** Artemis Racing Red with Outterridge at the helm. **» OPPOSITE BOTTOM** Artemis Racing team in Alameda, California, during the much-anticipated launch of their AC72 in November 2012.

When Italy's Mascalzone Latino stood down, citing Europe's economic downturn, Artemis Racing became the Challenger of Record for the 34th America's Cup. This could be heady stuff for a first-time challenger, but the team's CEO, Paul Cayard, brings a wealth of experience. The round-the-world race winner and 1998 U.S. Yachtsman of the Year crewed American hopefuls in 1983 as a trimmer and in 1987 as tactician. He skippered an Italian challenger in 1992 and then helmed the defender for skipper Dennis Conner in the 1995 loss to New Zealand. He skippered an American challenger in 2000, served as sports director for the Spanish team in 2007, and in 2009 joined Törnqvist's already successful Artemis Racing.

As training moved to developing the team's first AC72 and planning the next, Artemis brought in young Olympic 49er gold medalist Nathan Outteridge—whose short time as skipper of Team Korea had proved his abilities in wing-sailed catamarans—and Loïck Peyron, a charismatic salt with thirty-five years of big multihull experience. This pair, along with skipper Ian Percy, a top British sailor with two Olympic golds and one silver to his credit, came at the expense of Artemis Racing's first and principal skipper, Terry Hutchinson, who stepped aside in November 2012. "Terry gave nothing less than 110 percent," explained Cayard, but with unexpected hiccups in launching and sailing their first AC72, the team had to focus efforts on accelerating its program. In a sport Hutchinson himself explained as "a game of inches," something brought home when his team lost race seven by one second in the 2007 America's Cup, every decision, or indecision, counts. ♦

THE TEAM'S DNA EXTENDS all the way back to Fremantle in 1987 and the Kiwis' first attempt to win the America's Cup as New Zealand Challenge. They morphed into Team New Zealand in 1995, in San Diego, when *Black Magic* won the trophy in five straight races. Five years later New Zealand became the first country outside the United States to successfully defend. In 2007, with Dean Barker at the helm, a bit of rebranding, and Emirates as a partner, Emirates Team New Zealand (ETNZ) defeated Luna Rossa 5-0 to win the Louis Vuitton Cup finals and then won two of seven races in the America's Cup match against the defender, Alinghi. No other team at the 34th America's Cup has such a long, solid thread to its history.

The proud Royal New Zealand Yacht Squadron has probably produced more of the world's top sailors, per capita, than any other sailing institution—a cast

»BELOW LEFT Onboard Emirates Team New Zealand's AC72 with Dean Barker at the helm.

»BELOW RIGHT Emirates Team New Zealand was the first team to achieve full foiling capabilities with their AC72.

of characters ranging from Olympians to ocean racers to the best of America's Cup skippers.

New Zealand suffered a demoralizing inflection point in 2003, when the team lost the trophy. But that was then, and this is now. Under the guidance of battle-hardened Grant Dalton, a veteran of seven round-the-world races, ETNZ today operates as a disciplined cadre of professionals. They even have a business model. Significant funding comes from the government of New Zealand, which speaks volumes for the place that sailing holds in the hearts of the citizens of that country, and Emirates airline remains the lead sponsor.

ETNZ was the first team to launch an AC72 and the first to "lift off" on foils. With the move from monohulls to multihulls, Barker says, "We've moved from a world of detailing and fine-tuning to an open book with fresh, clean paper. There are no stupid questions or ideas. We're just scratching the surface of a huge, uncharted territory. You'll have to have your wits about you to get around the course, but Emirates Team New Zealand exists for the America's Cup. We've weathered the storm since 2007 to give ourselves the opportunity to compete in 2013." ♦

LUNA ROSSA CHALLENGE

BETWEEN THE GENESIS of America's Cup racing in the Solent on August 22, 1851, and the genesis of Luna Rossa's quest for the America's Cup lay a period of 145 years, five months, and twelve days. It happened in a moment of inspiration at a design meeting in Milan, not far from the marble Duomo that every visiting tourist knows. But for once, this design meeting in the fashion capital of Italy was not about couture. The chief executive of the house of Prada, lifelong sailor Patrizio Bertelli, meant to be shaping plans for a new cruising yacht when Argentinian designer Germán Frers exclaimed, "Why don't we do the America's Cup?"

In that moment, Prada Challenge was born, as was Luna Rossa, the team of the Red Moon. Bertelli could not know that, by 2013, he would become the first Italian inducted into the America's Cup Hall of Fame.

First, however, Prada would experience an unforgettable introduction to the game at the 2000 match in New Zealand. Eleven challengers from seven nations gathered to test their fortunes on the waters of the Hauraki Gulf. Skipper Francesco de Angelis won thirty-eight of forty-nine challenger races to claim the Louis Vuitton Cup on a high note. Then, in the America's Cup, came an 0–5 loss to the defenders, Team New Zealand, in their prime. It was a rousing opening act, nonetheless, the first occasion in which an American boat was absent from the America's Cup match. It was also the first outing in this arena for an Italian helmsman and a performance worthy of fashion house Prada's place on the world stage.

» **BELOW** Team Luna Rossa Challenge during the launch of their AC72. » **OPPOSITE** Luna Rossa Challenge at home on the historic waterways of Venice, Italy.

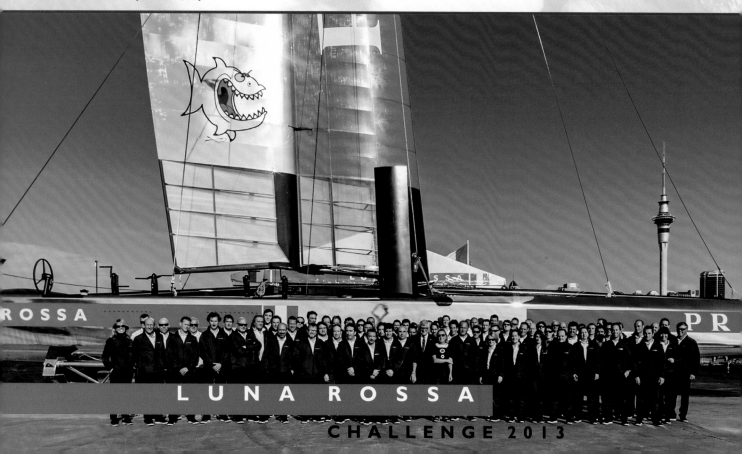

LUNA ROSSA

CHALLENGE 2013

Bertelli has fielded teams in each Louis Vuitton Cup since. In 2007, racing in Valencia, Spain, Luna Rossa made the final four. However, weighing the legal wrangling, delays, and bad blood that followed the 2007 races, he chose to wait on the sidelines until he could see AC45s on the water and a solid plan in place for racing on San Francisco Bay in AC72s. To reenter the game in 2011, leveraging a partnership with Emirates Team New Zealand, was a fortunate stroke for both. Luna Rossa poured in a welcome dose of funding, and the work already done on design and engineering by the Kiwis became available to the Italians. Luna Rossa's AC72 for the 2013 Louis Vuitton Cup shares the basic genetic code of the Kiwi boats. But, by rule, the teams went their separate ways in December 2012. The Italian boat answering the guns in 2013 is an Italian reinvention.

Looking back on his decision to jump into the fray and recommit to the time, the management headaches, and the extraordinary expenses, Bertelli recognized many motivations. Foremost, he said, "No Italian team was challenging. The Italian Challenger of Record had withdrawn its entry, and it was important to bring Italian sailing back to the position it always enjoyed internationally, and in the America's Cup in particular. Also, there were great expectations in a comeback of Luna Rossa. Over the years our team has won the affection and support of a very wide audience, and it has become a kind of Italian national team. I was also driven by a concern that skipping one Cup would have meant accumulating a huge technical delay. It would have made it more difficult to challenge for the following Cup."

Luna Rossa skipper Massimiliano "Max" Sirena has Cup fever as surely as anyone, it seems. He recalls winning the Louis Vuitton Cup in 2000 as a highlight of his life, but even greater than that was 2010, when Sirena trimmed the wing on BMW shore crew for ORACLE Racing's successful trimaran. "More than winning the race, on that day I drank Champagne from the Cup," Sirena recalled. "It's a feeling hard to describe. I was 'drugged' for a week."

Past Luna Rossa challenges carried the colors of yacht clubs from the central west coast and then the northern coast of Italy. This time out, Bertelli says, "After challenging with the Yacht Club Punta Ala and the Yacht Club Italiano, we have decided to challenge with the Circolo della Vela Sicilia, one of the oldest and most representative yacht clubs of Italian sailing. With this choice we wanted to underline and stress how much the presence of seamanship and sailing traditions on our peninsula—from the Liguria to the Venezia Giulia regions—is widespread and diverse." ◆

ORACLE TEAM USA represents a joining of powerful forces, plus a dose of serendipity. The team's owner, Larry Ellison, has the means, vision, and determination to drive change. The innovative CEO, Russell Coutts, has won more America's Cup races than anyone else. Coutts skippered for New Zealand in 1995 and 2000 and then for Switzerland in 2003 before masterminding the win in 2010 with BMW ORACLE Racing's giant trimaran. Jimmy Spithill, skipper of the tri and now the AC72, entered the game in 2000 at the age of twenty and has sailed in every Cup cycle since. At thirty, he was the youngest skipper to win an America's Cup. Tactician John "We're gonna have our hands full" Kostecki, inducted into the America's Cup Hall of Fame in 2012, is the only person who has won an Olympic medal, a race around the world, and the America's Cup. As a local, he's been swallowing San Francisco Bay salt water since Opti and El Toro prams looked big to a little guy.

Serendipity entered the equation in the early 2000s as word circulated around San Francisco that Ellison needed a yacht club he could represent as a challenger in New Zealand in 2003. At the time, the Golden Gate Yacht Club

» **BELOW** ORACLE TEAM USA at their home base at Pier 80 in San Francisco. » **OPPOSITE** *ORACLE TEAM USA 17* on San Francisco Bay.

was struggling financially, and Commodore Norbert Bajurin (returning to reprise the role in 2013) called a number at ORACLE and launched a story that will live forever in the annals of San Francisco sailing. Today the Golden Gate Yacht Club is the sixth trustee of the America's Cup and prospering from a big shot in the arm. Winning the America's Cup is like that. The club's team operates from a huge base at the Port of San Francisco's Pier 80, at the foot of Cesar Chavez Street, housing a stable of AC45s and, of course, two custom AC72s. One of those 72s, on September 7, 2013, will meet a challenger for race one of the 34th America's Cup, and a page will turn in the history of the Cup, which is also, to a great extent, the history of the sport of sailboat racing.

Ellison, in his role as defender, has left no stone unturned in building a successful defense effort, even while building a new framework around the competition that removes many of the advantages or perceived advantages that past defenders have enjoyed. He and Coutts pulled together a strong team of designers as well as a shore team that has found more than enough to keep them busy. "Keep 'em sailing" is the first mantra, and not the easiest.

As soon as he was clear of the 2012 Olympic Games and his fourth gold medal, Briton Ben Ainslie was brought in to begin training as a sparring partner for Jimmy Spithill. The two will race against each other in clashes between the two ORACLE boats, alternating with the race days of challengers competing in the Louis Vuitton Cup. Ainslie has designs on heading a British challenge for the 35th America's Cup, but for now he is part of a team that, however international in its origins, has been embraced by San Franciscans as their home team. Because it is. The defender. Sailing to keep the America's Cup in America. ♦

LAUNCHING

THE AC72s

The story of the San Francisco America's Cup is a story of bold decisions. Multihulls historically have been regarded as too slow through maneuvers for the elegant sparring of a proper match race. Ample tests were conducted before the decision was made to contest the America's Cup in catamarans.

Artemis Racing

» PAGES 72-73 After a
number of delays Artemis
Racing launched their first AC72
in November 2012. **» ABOVE**
Luna Rossa's AC72 in build.

The decision was controversial, and yes, something of the old game has been left behind, but much more has been brought forward. The 34th America's Cup will provide the ultimate test. To the objection that catamarans maneuver too slowly for match racing, Coutts replied, "That's because the right catamarans for match racing haven't been designed yet." As soon as the new breed of cats hit the water, it was clear that their time through maneuvers, from full speed to a return to full speed, was almost identical to the maneuvering times for the monohull International America's Cup Classic boats last raced in Valencia in 2007. The difference—the premium now on minimizing maneuvers—comes about because the other guy is going so fast while you're turning that you just can't give him any gimmes.

At the same time that catamarans were being trialed for match racing, the courses were shortened and constrained and moved closer and closer to shore, closer and closer to a potential audience, closer and closer to that day in 2012 when San Francisco's first America's Cup World Series wrapped up in the waters of the 2013 America's Cup match. Coutts, the cheers of the crowd still ringing in his ears, proclaimed yet another step complete, using words you've heard before, "Proof of concept!" The man who has won more America's Cup races than anyone else was pumped. The America's Cup World Series, the opening act of the 34th America's Cup, was getting rave reviews. Coutts had struggled through negativity, negativity, negativity, and now it was all fireworks. Curmudgeon-veterans of "the real America's Cup" were, even at that moment, adjusting their opinions in his favor. Now it all comes together, complete with surprises.

• • •

AFTER A YEAR of training and racing in smaller AC45s, four teams emerged as the true contenders for the 34th America's Cup. They are the teams, the defender and three challengers, that have built custom 72-footers, the weapon of choice for 2013. These are easily the fastest big boats ever to meet in competition, with the least predictable outcome in America's Cup history. Each launch was nervously anticipated. What would the designers make of the new, untested AC72 rule with its formulas that limit size but not innovation?

BOAT DIMENSIONS

AC45 PRINCIPAL DIMENSIONS

HULL LENGTH, 13.45 meters (44 feet)

MAXIMUM BEAM, 6.90 meters (22.6 feet)

MAST HEIGHT, 21.50 meters (70.5 feet)

MAXIMUM DRAFT, 2.70 meters (8.8 feet)

DISPLACEMENT, 1,400 kilograms (3,086 pounds)

WING AREA, 85 square meters (914 square feet)

JIB AREA, 48 square meters (516 square feet)

GENNAKER AREA, 125 square meters (1,345 square feet)

CREW, 5 people

AC72 PRINCIPAL DIMENSIONS

HULL LENGTH, 22 meters (72.2 feet)

MAXIMUM BEAM, 14 meters (45.9 feet)

MAST HEIGHT, 40 meters (131.2 feet)

MAXIMUM DRAFT, 4.40 meters (14.4 feet)

DISPLACEMENT, 5,900 kilograms (1,3007.2 pounds)

WING AREA, 260 square meters (2,798.6 square feet)

JIB AREA, 80 square meters (861.1 square feet)

GENNAKER AREA, 320 square meters (3,444.5 square feet)

CREW, 11 people

The 2013 rules do not allow teams to hide the boats once launched, but the design process is the equivalent of a state secret, with dozens of engineers and naval architects at work behind closed doors. Then come tens of thousands of hours of painstaking construction, laying carbon skin over honeycomb cores, creating complex parts that fit together in complex ways to make a highly complex machine that will carry eleven crewmen into the fight of their lives.

Emirates Team New Zealand was first in the water in the fall and the first to spring a surprise. New Zealand's designers had found a way to interpret the AC72 rule to unique advantage. From the get-go their boat employed hydrofoil-shaped daggerboards large enough to make the boat "fly" fully foiled—both hulls clear of the water—on the downwind legs. The speed gains are dramatic. With trimmable flaps prohibited (the rulemakers intended to prohibit foiling), the Kiwis had found a way to go foiling anyway by mounting the boards in cassettes and then trimming the cassettes to stabilize the boat.

Two teams immediately objected: ORACLE TEAM USA, the defender, and Artemis Racing, the Challenger of Record. The Italian challenger, Luna Rossa, did not object because the Italians have a design partnership with the Kiwis; their boat came out of the shed nearly identical to New Zealand's but punctuated with sleek mirrored surfaces and undeniable style. (Backed by the fashion house Prada, Luna Rossa's 72 is easily the most stylish of the breed.) The Kiwi system, with its large foiling daggerboards, and by extension the Italian system

THE WINGS TOWER 131 FEET ABOVE THE DECK—THE EQUIVALENT OF A THIRTEEN-STORY BUILDING.

» **BELOW** *ORACLE TEAM USA 17* about to roll out of the shed prior to launch in July 2012. » **RIGHT** For those who thought that multihulls couldn't possibly have the presence of monohulls, the launch of Luna Rossa's AC72 was revealing.

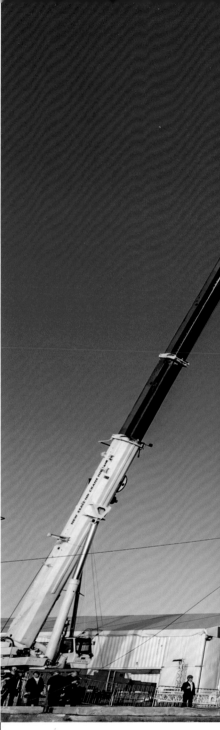

depend on an extra complication in the process of measurement, something that would not be allowed under a common-sense interpretation but which, the International Jury ruled, *is* allowed because it is not specifically prohibited.

Score one for the Kiwis and Italians? Probably. There remains the question of what is the fastest way to get around a tight racecourse with lots of maneuvers. Over the winter, the Kiwis occasionally had foiling issues upwind, and Matteo Plazzi, running Luna Rossa's performance program, openly wondered if "what makes you fast downwind could make you slow upwind."

ORACLE TEAM USA was the second to launch. Their first of two AC72s was capable of "flying" on its foils, but with smaller foils—dictated by their designers' common-sense interpretation of the rule—that needed more speed to lift the hulls clear of the water. Only Artemis launched a first boat without full-foil capability. The team did not comment on the reason.

• • •

IN THE FALL of 2012 ORACLE TEAM USA changed its training plans more than once, in the final case with the announced intention of "making some changes" to boat number one. Most observers assumed those changes would include larger foils. Then boat number one capsized, destroying the wing and requiring major renovation to the platform—not exactly the redesign opportunity the team had in mind. Artemis CEO Paul Cayard mused, "Imagine leaving the dock in the morning with a full kit of boat and coming home with fifty-five thousand man-hours of work ahead of you." To enter the September 2013 Cup match with confidence, the American team needs to have had their two boats on the water for months, tweaking for speed and learning how to sail in race conditions.

Each team is allowed to build three wings, and the defender used up one of those in the capsize. The wings can be as complicated as the engineers can imagine or as simple as a sailing team might prefer. With a wing developing as much as 40 percent more power per square foot than a soft sail and the wings towering 131 feet above the deck—the equivalent of a thirteen-story building, but very much "alive" with mechanical devices controlling shape—the teams have to expect to be overpowered much of the time. A smaller wing is not an option. The wiggle room for designers, the difference between maximum and minimum square footage, is only 2 percent.

As with hydrofoiling, these massive wings push the boundaries between maximum horsepower and horsepower that can be harnessed and used effectively. In either case, it's a lot. The way New Zealand team boss Grant Dalton tells it, "As soon as you put the wing in the boat and the boat in the water, it's trying to pull the dock away." ♦

» **BELOW** Emirates Team New Zealand foiling during an AC72 training session.

TACTICS

A

RACE IN AN AC72 CATAMARAN IS AN EMERGENCY THAT BEGINS AT THE START AND ENDS AT THE FINISH, IF THEN. IN THIRTY SECONDS

an AC72 can travel a third of a mile. "The fastest boats" is part of the mantra of the 34th America's Cup, and rightly so. But if you're riding that high-tech beast, if you're pulling on lines and reading wind-shifts and eyeing the competition and making bets in rapid order, you will be keenly aware of one additional fact. This is the shortest, tightest, most challenging race-course ever devised for an America's Cup. "Stadium sailing," the notion of presenting to a shoreside audience while imposing tight electronic boundaries around the

racecourse—keeping the boats together for the sake of the live audience and tele-vision audience alike—is a game changer.

At Valencia in 2007, it was common to see two monohull opponents split tacks at the start and sail off to opposite sides of the course, one going left and one going right, until they were *4 miles* apart, and come back together, close or even overlapped, at the top mark. It was a boatspeed contest played out at a fraction of the speeds of the 34th America's Cup, with differences between the boats measured in fractions of that fraction. In those days, a tactician spent most of his time standing in the back of the boat looking around, assessing meteorology, current flow, and position-ing relative to the other boat, and perhaps saying "We'll be tacking in thirty seconds, twenty-nine, twenty-eight . . ."

Well, forget that. In 2013, the tactician is also part of the steeplechase—never a whole two minutes without a maneuver—that keeps every crewmember's heart rate pumping full throttle. Before you can be a tactician in the 34th America's Cup, you must also be an athlete among athletes. And ready to adjust. The classic start, upwind to a mark dead upwind, has been around for generations. That's how everybody was trained, from Charlie Barr to Mike Vanderbilt to Bus Mosbacher, Ted Turner, Bill Ficker, Dennis Conner, John Bertrand, Russell Coutts, and Jimmy Spithill—and now it's gone. And that's only the start.

The new way of doing makes the race more of an attacking game, with more immediate passing opportunities and probably no safety for the leader. The race now opens with the wind blowing across

» **PAGES 80-81** The AC45s proved that catamarans could indeed round marks and maintain speed, an essential element to the close and exciting racing promised for the America's Cup match. » **BELOW** Artemis Racing White amid ships during an ACWS fleet race.

the boat from the starboard (right) side. In the lingo, it's a "reaching start," with the boats on their fastest point of sail. At the two-minute mark of a two-minute countdown—don't be over the start line before the countdown reaches zero—the opponents enter the starting area from opposite sides, and already there is a dynamic.

To a sailor, the world is wind. Where the wind is coming from is upwind. Where it is blowing to is downwind. Everything that matters happens in this dimension. The sailor inhabits the wind by instinct, feels it in the hairs on the neck, sees its effect on the surface of the water, and feels it in the reaction of the boat. At every moment, depending on the boats' positioning relative to the wind and relative to each other, one boat has the right-of-way. As they maneuver, the right-of-way advantage can shift rapidly and dramatically. That is the drama of the prestart dance.

On the countdown clock, from their opposite sides, both boats cross the start line and enter the start box with two minutes to go. One is required to

enter on starboard tack, with right-of-way, and the other is required to enter on port tack as the give-way vessel. The Race Committee will position the marks to allow a well-handled give-way vessel a reasonable chance of making a clean, clear crossing in front of its opponent. If the give-way boat can successfully cross in front, its disadvantage is neutralized, and the game is on. If it fails to cross, the game is on anyway. Welcome to the jungle.

John Kostecki, tactician to ORACLE TEAM USA, says, "Coming in on port tack, whether or not you can get across the other guy depends on just how the line is set, and what the wind does, and of course getting the timing right. If you make it across, you have the freedom to decide when you want to come back and approach the line. The other guy will have to decide whether he thinks you're late or early. If you're late, he'll want to go in front of you. If you're early, he'll want to go behind."

It's a two-boat race, so the critical thing is to be ahead of the other boat, preferably at the start but especially rounding

» **ABOVE** Luna Rossa Challenge (right) and Emirates Team New Zealand (left) spar on their 72s during a training session in New Zealand.

THE SAILOR INHABITS

the wind by instinct, feels it in the hairs on the neck, sees its effect on the surface of the water, and feels it in the reaction of the boat.

the first mark and entering the open legs of the course. Between the start and mark one, the reach is a mad dash, mere seconds, that more often than not favors the boat to leeward, on the left, which will be the "inside" boat at the rounding. Often, the prestart maneuvering is about claiming that position and asserting control. "You look for the spot on the start line that is shortest distance to the mark, on your fastest point of sail," Kostecki says. "If you get that, and you're tight to leeward of the other boat, that's ideal. On such a short leg there is no way they're going to sail all the way around you and pass."

There are other possibilities. Sail enough races, and there will be times when one boat separates upwind and has a faster angle to the mark (*leverage* is the sailor's term) and gets there first. Not often, but it happens. With only two minutes on the countdown, inside the start

box, the decisions come fast and furious.

The shape of the new America's Cup course developed through experiments in AC45 class racing over the last two years. That reaching start would have been heresy just a few years ago. It is unique to the 34th America's Cup. The main portions of the course are more familiar to racing sailors: At the top and bottom of the course is a "gate," and each gate consists of two marks a distance apart. The tactician can choose to round either mark and go left or go right. One mark or the other will always represent a way to minimize maneuvers and maximize speed, but perhaps there is a reason to go the other way. Perhaps one side of the course has better wind or current, enough to pay off an extra tack or jibe. Or perhaps, no matter what else is going on, it is absolutely necessary to get away from a boat ahead and roll the dice by sailing in a different patch of water.

» **BELOW** The AC72s are designed to have an enormous amount of grinding input. Here eight ORACLE TEAM USA members grind a single winch.
» **OPPOSITE** With the AC45s, it was about finessing the tiller. Nathan Outteridge at the helm of Artemis Racing Red's AC45.

ORACLE TEAM USA (17)

By multihull standards, AC72s maneuver well. Even so, every tack and every jibe slows the boat and costs distance. An important feature of the tactician's job is to minimize maneuvers. If he can force the other boat to make an extra maneuver, that's huge. The no-brainer way to minimize maneuvers is to sail all the way to the electronic boundary of the course before making a turn, but there is no such thing as a no-brainer strategy that will get you all the way around the course. Luna Rossa's Francesco Bruni sees a stark comparison to the monohull racing at Valencia in 2007, where there were "perhaps twenty decision points between the start and the finish. If you made a mistake, there was a chance that you could make a couple of tacks or a jibe and correct it. Now, there are half that many decision points, and each decision is weighted heavily. If there is a windshift that persuades you to not go to the boundary, then you probably will be bouncing from that point on. If it's a mistake, you will have to live with it to the next decision point. You can't just change your mind and throw in a couple of extra tacks. The price outweighs any possible benefit."

The imperative is to minimize maneuvers, and with that in mind, we can reel this account back to the first mark and consider why, most of the time, a boat will turn downwind without jibing and head for the right-hand side of the course (looking downwind). Simply put, that's the fast way to go. Even the trailing boat is likely to take that route, unless its tactician sees a big-stakes advantage in wind direction or wind strength on the left-hand side of the course. Such an advantage would have to be worth at least three or preferably four boatlengths to justify the cost of the maneuver. Water flow could also force a decision. With one-sixth of all the water in San Francisco Bay going out and in twice a day, currents are power-

ful, more so than in most places where boats race. If there is a 3-knot differential in water flow between the left and right sides of the course, the tactician probably cannot ignore it, even if his boat is going 30 knots (3 knots being one-tenth of 30). If the trailing boat jibes at the first mark and goes left, the lead boat can cover the move or not, but if the trailing boat jibes to match, it probably will settle in for a few seconds first, rather than slam the maneuver. "If there's any doubt," says Kostecki, "go to the boundaries."

No one wants to break the electronic boundaries of the course—that's a costly foul—but everything about the 34th America's Cup is pushing the boundaries of sailing. These are boats that are capable of flipping end over end. These are boats that will show closing speeds of 60, 70, 80 miles per hour. This is a new world, and with a final reaching leg to the finish line from the bottom of the course, the races finish for the crowd and the cameras "around the corner" at Pier 27, where the press awaits them, and the fans, and happiness or failure. Once upon a time, Dennis Conner became the most famous sailor in the world by losing the America's Cup. That's off the table. The only option now is to win. ♦

An important feature of the tactician's job is to minimize maneuvers. If he can force the other boat to make an extra maneuver, *THAT'S HUGE.*

SAILING ON THE EDGE: THE DANGER

SAILING HAS ALWAYS HAD ITS DANGERS. Look around any Grand Prix regatta and count the number of people with missing fingers or fingertips. This is an occupational hazard where lines and structures are under severe load. Head injuries, particularly from the boom sweeping violently across the boat, sometimes have fatal consequences. Drownings from falling overboard or being trapped in the rigging of an overturned boat are uncommon but not unheard of.

All these dangers remain a presence on the America's Cup catamarans, but there are additional threats. The speed of the boats alone heightens the possibility of injury. Capsizing is the most common accident so far, but there have been numerous collisions, some with boats riding up and over rival boats in the heat of crowded mark roundings.

In the August 2012 San Francisco regatta, Russell Coutts lived up to a long-standing reputation as "Crash Coutts" when he rammed the Race Committee boat after charging into a crowded start line and finding no place to go. "There was no gap there and it was too late to do anything about it," he explained before joking with the shore crew not to repair the damage too well, because it might happen again.

The crash threatened both Coutts's crew and the officials on the committee boat. Yet Coutts had the presence of mind to make a course alteration to hit the committee boat square on, minimizing the damage to his AC45. If he turned-up and made a glancing hit, he might have knocked the bow clean off his port hull.

No one was injured, but a portion of the ORACLE's starboard bow was left impaled in the side of the committee boat. "We were not able to extract it, so we covered it over," said Regatta Director Iain Murray with a shrug. He suggested it might have even added value to the injured boat: "When carbon is compressed like that, you make a diamond."

Cup teams had become used to capsizing the smaller AC45 catamarans used in the America's Cup World Series regattas and adept at quickly recovering them. A kind of "capsize culture" had developed where these accidents were almost celebrated as part of the general entertainment. However, while a cheerful gung-ho attitude toward the crowd-pleasing crash culture developed with the AC45s, the much bigger and more powerful AC72s are a different proposition.

〉〉〉〉〉

WHEN IT WAS time to choose a venue for the 34th America's Cup, San Francisco Bay was touted as the ideal showcase for racing, a natural amphitheater for live viewing with reliable, big winds and dramatic, camera-pleasing backdrops. All elements were in play early on the afternoon of October 16, 2012. With two successful regattas in the bag in smaller boats, ORACLE TEAM USA was confidently making fast tracks across the bay in their new 72-foot catamaran. It was only the eighth day of testing for the first of ORACLE TEAM USA's two AC72s, and it was attracting plenty of attention from a crowd of race-goers on the city front. They were there to watch a different regatta but were drawn to the dazzling speed of the big cat.

The San Francisco Bay sea breeze builds throughout the afternoon. That's a rule. And the defending America's Cup team may have stayed out just a bit too long. With the breeze at 25 knots, gusting higher, it was time to head for the barn. Jimmy Spithill was at the helm, making fast tracks to weather, but...

» **PAGES 86-87** Emirates Team New Zealand speeding through heavy chop. Exposed, fast, and slippery, the AC45s and AC72s require a new approach to safety—you won't see crew sailing them in heavy conditions without crash helmets and form-fitting flotation and impact vests. » **OPPOSITE** Emirates Team New Zealand capsized during the first day of America's Cup World Series racing in Newport, Rhode Island, and struggled for nearly an hour to right their boat. » **ABOVE** Fitness became an essential part of the 34th America's Cup, both for sailing the fast, demanding boats and shaking off quick and violent capsizes.

"WHEN CARBON IS COMPRESSED LIKE THAT, YOU MAKE A DIAMOND."

IT HAPPENED. THE UNTHINKABLE. WITH SPITHILL YELLING "KEEP AN EYE ON YOUR MATES!" THE BOAT WENT OVER AND DOWN IN A HAIL OF SPRAY.

The boat had to turn around and head downwind to go home. That turn, the bear-away as sailors call it, is the danger point in catamaran sailing. The power driving the wing goes up dramatically. Only more boatspeed can absorb that driving force, but it takes time to build speed. Meanwhile, the wing wants to push the bows down and bury them deep. Deep. Deeper.

It happened. The unthinkable. With Spithill yelling "Keep an eye on your mates!" the boat went over and down in a hail of spray. The pitchpole and, ultimately, the capsize of ORACLE's first AC72 catamaran fulfilled the "death and destruction" predictions of doomsayers and served as a wake-up call to all four teams sailing AC72s in 2013. Reliable wind makes for reliable race scheduling, and San Francisco Bay delivers. Big wind makes for big excitement, and San Francisco Bay delivers. The headlands surrounding that striking red bridge are scenic, but the Golden Gate Strait funnels and intensifies the wind and tide. It's a ride—a ride and a half. Many lessons were learned, not the least of which is that team members—even after ample experience righting smaller capsized boats—were not able to get an AC72 back on its feet in a hurry.

The result was catastrophic. The wing structure holds air, so the wing is a flotation device, but only as long as it holds together. With an ebb-tide current running seaward at better than 5 knots—a fast walking pace, or a moderate jog—the boat was still on its ear when it was swept under the bridge and into the white-capped chop in the strait. Outside the bay, in the maelstrom, the situation was hopeless, a reminder of the Homeric phrase *the gobbly sea*. It was touch and go for the entire boat, Spithill said, as

the wing broke up by degrees, and the boat completed its capsize. The wreckage was pulled 6 miles beyond the bridge before the tide began to turn. Inbound currents then helped the salvage crew, working slowly in the dark, in the wee hours of the new day, as they towed the overturned platform through the Golden Gate and home.

Stunned was the word from many, including team CEO Russell Coutts. So much for the thirty days of practice allowed in 2012. So much for getting ahead of the learning curve with a tricky new machine, and so much for looking awesome. The platform was repairable, the wing was gone, and each team is allowed only three wings. The prospect of relaunching with wing number two, then testing and training with platform number two and wing number three, left the American defenders of the Cup no room for a repeat performance.

The challengers could read their own lessons there, especially Luna Rossa with its one-boat program that could be "over," literally, in a moment should the boat capsize in a race for the Louis Vuitton Cup. With the crash of ORACLE TEAM USA, what everyone knew in theory became hard reality. The heat is on, and the extreme safety measures undertaken by all the teams are justified. Medical staff in the chase boats. Divers ready to hit the water in an instant. A personal supply of oxygen for each of the crew, in case they are trapped under an overturned boat. Knives to cut through the netting. Training days in a pool, jumping off a thirty-foot height or swimming fifty feet underwater like commandos. You can still call it "yacht racing," but no one imagines the 34th America's Cup as business as usual. ♦

» **PAGES 90-91** Team Korea powers through the heavy waters of San Francisco Bay while the afternoon sun casts a brilliant light on their efforts.
» **OPPOSITE AND ABOVE** The capsize of *ORACLE TEAM USA 17* was both dramatic and dangerous. Fortunately, despite pitchpoling at more than 30 knots and being dragged out to sea for hours, no one was injured.

THE RED BULL
YOUTH AMERICA'S CUP

THE RED BULL YOUTH AMERICA'S CUP is a new event under the umbrella of the 34th America's Cup and is intended to afford young, talented sailors a clear pathway towards competing for one of the most prestigious trophies in sport – the America's Cup.

In years past youth sailors have had a difficult task ascending the hierarchy of an America's Cup team. Youth sailors simply weren't viewed as having enough experience to compete at the high level demanded by America's Cup crews. The Red Bull Youth America's Cup aims to shatter that glass ceiling.

The Red Bull Youth America's Cup is open to national teams of six sailors, aged 19 to 24 in 2013. Each crew must hold a valid passport of the country their team represents. Equipment, including the AC45 platform and wing sail – the same as used in the America's Cup World Series – will be supplied to participating teams.

Teams had two different opportunities to qualify for the RBYAC. Teams that gained the backing of an official America's Cup World Series team automatically qualified for the September finale, upon approval from the regatta director. Five teams took this path.

Five other teams qualified through a selection series in February 2013, comprised of two seven-day sessions. Red Bull sailing directors Roman Hagara and Hans-Peter Steinacher, double Olympic Gold medalists, selected the teams for the finale based on their performance at the selection series.

"This is a great opportunity to observe the youth teams train and compete under high-pressure situations during the selection camp," said Hagara, a two-time Olympic gold medalist in the Tornado catamaran. "It's a fantastic way to assess who can perform to their best and to select those who deserve to qualify for the main event."

Of the 10 teams in the finale, two are American teams selected by ORACLE TEAM USA, the reigning America's Cup champion. The two teams are USA45 Racing (representing the U.S.) and American Youth Sailing Force (representing the San Francisco Bay Area).

"It's honestly the most amazing feeling ever," said USA45 Racing trimmer and team manager Jacob La Dow (San Diego, California/St. Mary's College of Maryland). "It's a dream come true."

Joseph Phelps

INSIGNIA

NAPA VALLEY

ESTATE GROWN

RED WINE

Napa Valley

The Official Wine Region
of the 34th America's Cup

Napa Valley long ago established itself as a destination when steamships began traveling the three-hour trip from San Francisco to the city of Napa via the Napa River. A railroad line soon became available from the ferry terminal at Vallejo on the shores of San Pablo Bay to the city of Calistoga, creating new access to the healing waters of Calistoga's famed geothermal hot springs. The Napa Valley has weathered some tough times in its relatively short history. The Valley's once-famed Silverado Mine was exhausted in 1875 after just three years of operation. In 1893 an outbreak of phylloxera, a serious grapevine disease, crippled many of the Valley's 140 wineries.

Prohibition, enacted in 1920, dealt the final blow to the early wine industry. Only a handful of wineries survived the thirteen years of Prohibition by producing sacramental wines and selling grapes to home winemakers. Today, however, with vision and perseverance, the industry has greatly surpassed its earlier "golden age," and now boasts more than 400 wineries, producing some of the world's finest wines.

The Napa Valley continues to be a thriving agricultural area, a unique characteristic within the San Francisco Bay Area. This is thanks to a group of concerned citizens who in 1968 had the foresight to create the first Agricultural Preserve in the United States. A land zoning ordinance voted on by a majority of the county's citizens established agriculture and open space as the "best use" for the land within Napa County. The "Ag Preserve" designates more than 438,000 acres (177,300 hectares) within Napa County as agricultural preserve or watershed protection lands.

Now home to more than 400 wineries, 125 restaurants with twelve Michelin stars (more than any other wine region), and 150 hotels and inns, Napa Valley is the wine, food, arts, and wellness capital of North America.

NAPA VALLEY

At every turn, awe-inspiring natural beauty unfolds in the Napa Valley, America's first agricultural preserve, where the highest standards for farming excellence, healthy community and gracious hospitality are the cornerstones of daily life. You'll want to stay a little longer.

SailNapaValley.com

34 SAN FRANCISCO 2013
AMERICA'S
CUP

Official wine region of the
34th America's Cup

LIFESTYLE
PROPERTIES

St. Helena Vineyard and Estate site, $3.8 mi

LIFESTYLE
PROPERTIES

Napa Valley's Go-To Realtor®

LOUIS VUITTON CUP
AMERICA'S CUP CHALLENGER SERIES

34 AMERICA'S CUP
SAN FRANCISCO 2013

	MONDAY	TUESDAY	WEDNESDAY	THURSDAY	FRIDAY	SATURDAY	SUNDAY
JULY				**4 JULY** Opening Day	**5 JULY** Fleet Racing for Challengers and Defender	**6 JULY**	**7 JULY** Louis Vuitton Cup Round Robin 1
	8 JULY Reserve Day	**9 JULY** Louis Vuitton Cup Round Robin 1	**10 JULY** Louis Vuitton Cup Round Robin 1	**11 JULY** Reserve Day	**12 JULY** Louis Vuitton Cup Round Robin 2	**13 JULY** Louis Vuitton Cup Round Robin 2	**14 JULY** Louis Vuitton Cup Round Robin 2
	15 JULY Reserve Day	**16 JULY** Louis Vuitton Cup Round Robin 3	**17 JULY** Louis Vuitton Cup Round Robin 3	**18 JULY** Reserve Day	**19 JULY** Louis Vuitton Cup Round Robin 3	**20 JULY** Louis Vuitton Cup Round Robin 4	**21 JULY** Louis Vuitton Cup Round Robin 4
	22 JULY Reserve Day	**23 JULY** Louis Vuitton Cup Round Robin 4	**24 JULY** Louis Vuitton Cup Round Robin 5	**25 JULY** Reserve Day	**26 JULY** Louis Vuitton Cup Round Robin 5	**27 JULY** Louis Vuitton Cup Round Robin 5	**28 JULY** Louis Vuitton Cup Round Robin 6
	29 JULY Reserve Day	**30 JULY** Louis Vuitton Cup Round Robin 6	**31 JULY** Louis Vuitton Cup Round Robin 6	**1 AUGUST** Reserve Day	**2 AUGUST** Louis Vuitton Cup Round Robin 7	**3 AUGUST** Louis Vuitton Cup Round Robin 7	**4 AUGUST** Louis Vuitton Cup Round Robin 7
AUGUST	**5 AUGUST** Reserve Day	**6 AUGUST** Louis Vuitton Cup Semi Final	**7 AUGUST** Louis Vuitton Cup Semi Final	**8 AUGUST** Reserve Day	**9 AUGUST** Louis Vuitton Cup Semi Final	**10 AUGUST** Louis Vuitton Cup Semi Final	**11 AUGUST** Louis Vuitton Cup Semi Final*
	12 AUGUST Reserve Day	**13 AUGUST** Louis Vuitton Cup Semi Final*	**14 AUGUST** Louis Vuitton Cup Semi Final*	**15 AUGUST** Reserve Day	**16 AUGUST** Reserve Day	**17 AUGUST** LVC Final Race 1 LVC Final Race 2	**18 AUGUST** LVC Final Race 3 LVC Final Race 4
	19 AUGUST Reserve Day	**20 AUGUST** Non-Race Day	**21 AUGUST** LVC Final Race 5 LVC Final Race 6	**22 AUGUST** Reserve Day	**23 AUGUST** Reserve Day	**24 AUGUST** LVC Final Race 7 LVC Final Race 8*	**25 AUGUST** LVC Final Race 9* LVC Final Race 10*
	26 AUGUST Reserve Day	**27 AUGUST** Non-Race Day	**28 AUGUST** LVC Final Race 11* LVC Final Race 12*	**29 AUGUST** Reserve Day	**30 AUGUST** Louis Vuitton Cup Final Race 13*	**31 AUGUST** Reserve Day	**1 SEPTEMBER** Red Bull Youth America's Cup
SEPTEMBER	**2 SEPTEMBER** Red Bull Youth America's Cup	**3 SEPTEMBER** Red Bull Youth America's Cup	**4 SEPTEMBER** Red Bull Youth America's Cup	**5 SEPTEMBER** Non-Race Day	**6 SEPTEMBER** Non-Race Day	**7 SEPTEMBER** America's Cup Race 1 Race 2	**8 SEPTEMBER** America's Cup Race 3 Race 4
	9 SEPTEMBER Superyacht Regatta	**10 SEPTEMBER** America's Cup Race 5 Race 6	**11 SEPTEMBER** Superyacht Regatta	**12 SEPTEMBER** America's Cup Race 7 Race 8	**13 SEPTEMBER** Superyacht Regatta	**14 SEPTEMBER** America's Cup Race 9 Race 10*	**15 SEPTEMBER** America's Cup Race 11* Race 12*
	16 SEPTEMBER Reserve Day	**17 SEPTEMBER** America's Cup Race 13* Race 14*	**18 SEPTEMBER** Reserve Day	**19 SEPTEMBER** America's Cup Race 15* Race 16*	**20 SEPTEMBER** Reserve Day	**21 SEPTEMBER** America's Cup Race 17*	**22 SEPTEMBER** Reserve Day
	23 SEPTEMBER Reserve Day	**24 SEPTEMBER**	**25 SEPTEMBER**	**26 SEPTEMBER**	**27 SEPTEMBER**	**28 SEPTEMBER**	**29 SEPTEMBER**

LVC = Louis Vuitton Cup, America's Cup Challenger Series

RR = Round Robin

* = Racing if necessary

INSIGHT
EDITIONS

PO Box 3088
San Rafael, CA 94912
www.insighteditions.com

f Find us on Facebook: www.facebook.com/InsightEditions
t Follow us on Twitter: @insighteditions

Library of Congress Cataloging-in-Publication Data available.

ISBN: 978-1-60887-248-0

ROOTS OF PEACE   REPLANTED PAPER

Insight Editions, in association with Roots of Peace, will plant two trees for each tree
used in the manufacturing of this book. Roots of Peace is an internationally renowned
humanitarian organization dedicated to eradicating land mines worldwide and
converting war-torn lands into productive farms and wildlife habitats. Roots of Peace
will plant two million fruit and nut trees in Afghanistan and provide farmers there with
the skills and support necessary for sustainable land use.

Book design by Jenelle Wagner

Manufactured in China by Insight Editions

10 9 8 7 6 5 4 3 2 1

PHOTO CREDITS: © ACEA: 21 (top), 50, 51 (middle), 75; © Carlo
Borlenghi / Luna Rossa Challenge: 10, 20, 57 (bottom), 68-9, 72-3, 74,
77, 102; © Chris Cameron: 4-5, 14-5, 22, 66-7, 78; © Sharon Green: 13, 19,
24-5, 36-7, 38 (top), 39, 60, 90-1; © Guilain Grenier / ORACLE TEAM
USA: 2-3, 6-7, 12, 42-3, 70-1, 76, 84, 86-7, 92, 93; © Gilles Martin-Raget /
ACEA: 1, 8-9, 11, 27 (top), 28-9, 30-3, 38 (bottom), 44-5, 47, 49, 51 (top),
52-3, 54, 55, 56-7 (top), 58, 64 (bottom), 80-1, 82, 85, 88, 94; © Sander van
der Borch: 18, 62-3, 64 (top), 65, 72-3, 77, 89, 103-4

ADDITIONAL CREDITS: © Peter Beren ("The Golden Gate").
All rights reserved. Used with permission; © Guilain Grenier: 17;
© Ivor Wilkins / ACEA: 21; Courtesy of San Francisco Maritime National
Historic Park: 26-7; © Morton Beebe: 34; © Dan Nerney: 38 (middle);
© Daniel Forster: 40; © Gilles Martin-Raget: 41; © Voltaire Yap: 46;
© Luna Rossa Challenge / Nigel Marpel: 48, 83